The
Golden
Future

Also by Diana Cooper

Books

The Magic of Unicorns (2020)

Dragons (2018)

The Archangel Guide to the Animal World (2017)

The Archangel Guide to Enlightenment and Mastery (2016)

The Archangel Guide to Ascension (2015)

Venus: A Diary of a Puppy and Her Angel (2014)

Oracle Card Decks

The Magic of Unicorns (2021)

Archangel Oracle Cards (2020)

Archangel Animal Oracle Cards (2019)

Dragon Oracle Cards (2017)

Audio Visualizations

The Magic of Unicorns (2020)

Dragons (2018)

The Archangel Guide to Enlightenment and Mastery (2016)

The Archangel Guide to Ascension (2015)

The
Golden
Future

What to Expect and How to Reach the Fifth Dimension

DIANA COOPER

HAY HOUSE

Carlsbad, California • New York City
London • Sydney • New Delhi

Published in the United Kingdom by:
Hay House UK Ltd, The Sixth Floor, Watson House
54 Baker Street, London W1U 7BU
Tel: +44 (0)20 3927 7290; Fax: +44 (0)20 3927 7291
www.hayhouse.co.uk

Published in the United States of America by:
Hay House Inc., PO Box 5100, Carlsbad, CA 92018-5100
Tel: (1) 760 431 7695 or (800) 654 5126
Fax: (1) 760 431 6948 or (800) 650 5115; www.hayhouse.com

Published in Australia by:
Hay House Australia Ltd, 18/36 Ralph St, Alexandria NSW 2015
Tel: (61) 2 9669 4299; Fax: (61) 2 9669 4144; www.hayhouse.com.au

Published in India by:
Hay House Publishers India, Muskaan Complex,
Plot No.3, B-2, Vasant Kunj, New Delhi 110 070
Tel: (91) 11 4176 1620; Fax: (91) 11 4176 1630; www.hayhouse.co.in

A catalogue record for this book is available from the British Library.

Tradepaper ISBN: 978-1-4019-7287-5
E-book ISBN: 978-1-78817-937-9
Audiobook ISBN: 978-1-78817-938-6

Interior illustrations: 1, 35, 133, 219: Space Before; all other illustrations: Shutterstock

11 10 9 8 7 6 5 4 3

Printed in the United States of America

This product uses papers sourced from responsibly managed forests.
For more information, see www.hayhouse.com.

Contents

Part III   Preparing for the Fifth Dimension

Part I

The Journey to the Golden Future of Earth

Chapter 1

Your Invitation to Earth

Earth is a special mystery school. The lessons and understandings offered are unique. You are amazingly blessed to receive the opportunity to be here. Rejoicing in a rainbow, examining a butterfly, stroking a cat, touching a petal, smelling a flower, paddling in a stream or playing with a child are sensations only available on Earth.

When Lady Gaia invites you here, she reminds you that life on Earth is a unique opportunity. Be grateful for it. You are a spiritual being who has volunteered for this expedition.

One of the items of equipment you receive is a physical body, connected to your emotional and mental bodies. Your mind, emotions and physical body are delicate feedback instruments. Everything comes through your spiritual body and filters into your mind. Your thoughts affect your emotions as well as your physical wellbeing. Your emotions are also reflected in your health and body. You are expected to pay attention to this.

You are also equipped with a team of helpers. After all, if you are exploring foreign terrain, even if you have been there several times before, you will need your team to scout ahead, to help you search for food and shelter, and to draw your attention to those things you have come to explore or learn.

These helpers are your guides and angels, especially your guardian angel, who has been with you throughout your soul journey. This is the being, usually invisible to you, who encourages you, protects you, tries to point out the right path and arranges for you to meet the people you need to connect with in order to fulfil your destiny.

There are also many other angels and archangels who are with you the instant you need them. Remember to ask for help, for they cannot assist you unless you ask, as it would contravene your free will.

In addition, you have guides, who have usually but not always experienced an incarnation on Earth. These can change as you progress on your path. If, for example, you decide to become a solicitor, a guide will come to you who can help you with the law. If you train to be a medical professional, a healing guide will assist you. You can have several guides.

An incarnation on Earth is considered to be the Everest of experiences. If you are climbing that particular mountain, you need a good team of sherpas. And it massively enhances and assists your journey if you consult them!

Every year on your birthday, Lady Gaia's angels sing over you with love to renew the welcome of your invitation. They also check that the blueprint for your life is still right for you. Do you need to change the original design? Does it still fulfil the vision you held when you incarnated?

Every seventh year, your overlighting archangel consults your guardian angel to see how your mission is progressing. If you need support or help, this will be provided. This also applies if you have moved onto a different path or progressed even more than envisaged.

Your soul chose your name because it had a specific vibration that aligned with your mission. Every time it is sounded, it calls in your soul lessons. On your birthday, the angels sing in the vibration of your full name with great love in order to encourage you. If alterations need to be made to your life path, this will be reflected in the vibrations of the angelic voices.

All these lessons, instructions and experiences are brought to you through your spiritual energy centres, or chakras. As we move into the fifth dimension and our 12 chakras are established, the lessons become more advanced and more precise. We are moving from school to university.

Later on, I will be sharing the lessons you need to understand, experience or master in each chakra. When you have mastered the lessons of the 12 spiritual centres, you can integrate your divine master blueprint and start to bring back your gifts and your divine wisdom as we move forward into the golden future.

VISUALIZATION TO CONNECT WITH YOUR ANGELS AND GUIDES

- Sit quietly and relax.

- See or sense your guardian angel beside you.

- See or sense how many other angels are with you.

- See or sense your guides with you.

- Invoke your overlighting archangel and see or sense them with you.

- How does it feel to have so much help and guidance?

- Ask any questions and sense the response.

Chapter 2

The Golden Future of Earth

Between 2012 and 2032 Earth is birthing a new fifth-dimensional Golden Age, a period during which everything will radiate a golden aura of love and wisdom. It commences in 2032, and the world will have changed beyond recognition by that time.

It is destined that our planet and everyone on her will be fifth-dimensional (or at least at the upper levels of the fourth dimension) by 2032. How we experience this transition is up to us, but Earth itself will ascend fully into the fifth dimension in 2032, whether or not individuals stay for the ride.

If you are reading these words, you have incarnated to help the planet make this transition. It is a responsibility and also a massive opportunity for ascension.

*The current period, between 2012 and
2032, is the most important that there has
ever been in the history of the planet.*

We are at a crucial stage.

Therefore, it is really important to listen to and act on your intuition. Only listen to positive predictions and messages. Give no energy to anything else. Focus on the new and wonderful awaiting you when you arrive at the end of the journey. If you do this, your aura will become more and more golden.

> *During the 20 years between 2012 and*
> *2032, a metamorphosis will take place.*

Some events during this 20-year period are set in stone; for example, the Olympic Games were always going to be held in London in 2012, regardless of how much bidding or competition there was from other cities around the world. London is the Earth Star chakra of Earth, and the energy and excitement of the Olympic Games were needed to activate it, for it is only when this chakra awakens, in an individual or a planet, that the ascension process can start.

Some of your own experiences, too, are predestined. These may include, for example, meeting your partner or travelling to a certain country. If something is preordained, it will happen no matter what. However, your thoughts, actions and visualizations can massively influence your life journey, including your fated relationships and life events.

> *Currently, your thoughts, attitudes and visualizations*
> *are helping to co-create a new Golden Age. When you*
> *energize the predictions for the golden future, you are*
> *manifesting the new world in the best possible way.*

The end of a cycle

Let's put the significance of the years between 2012 and 2032 into perspective. The year 2012 marked the end of a 26,000-year cosmic era. It was also the end of a cycle of 10 cosmic eras, so it finalized a 260,000-year epoch for all the universes.

A cosmic epoch is sometimes called an out-breath of God, and this is a period of creation. It is followed by a 20-year in-breath of God, when the outmoded collapses and anything that is not working is drawn back to the Godhead. We are in the middle of this stage right now. In 2032 a new out-breath of creation will begin at a frequency higher than before.

For 260,000 years, Earth was part of a fourth-dimensional universe. However, Earth itself was third-dimensional. Of all the planets in this universe, Earth alone descended to the lower frequency.

During this vast epoch, for 1,500 years, the legendary Golden Era of Atlantis arose like a light in the darkness. In that period, everyone was fifth-dimensional and acted for the highest good of all. It was a time of contentment, happiness and extraordinary crystal technology.

Then one powerful mage decided to use his power for his own benefit. He used it to control others and his lower consciousness spread quickly. People closed their hearts and became self-centred. The frequency of Atlantis rapidly devolved into the third dimension. Higher beings who were helping had to withdraw, as they could not access such a low vibration. Five chakras containing the gifts of the Atlanteans were withdrawn from humanity. Finally, the Intergalactic Council decided to terminate that period in a great flood.

In the 10,000 years that followed, third-dimensional Earth underwent a new experiment, that of masculine domination.

Why was Earth third-dimensional in a fourth-dimensional universe?

There are two reasons why our planet was out of step with the rest of our universe. The first is that ages ago a call went out from the Intergalactic Council to all the planets to volunteer to host a unique experiment, that of free will. People could choose whether to act from their divine will or their lower one. Throughout the cosmos, nothing like this had ever been considered, and the concept was regarded with awe, wonder and amazement by every being in the universes.

The Council for Planet Earth volunteered for the experiment. Souls daring to incarnate would go through the Veil of Amnesia, forget that they were divine beings and step into the unknown.

Another agreement of the free-will experiment was that every thought and action would be recorded, and if the balance sheet of a lifetime was in debit, the soul agreed to incarnate again to try to balance their karmic account.

Over the years, beings from all over the universes have been watching in awe and amazement the courageous adventurers who have dared to incarnate as humans on Earth. Anyone who enters this planet is considered exceptionally brave. It is regarded as a jungle where you face many challenges to your soul. If you meet a being out in the cosmos who learns that you have been to Earth, they will look at you with respect and admiration!

No one expected those on Earth to sink into self-centred, selfish behaviour, but we did. While the remainder of this universe remained open-hearted and fourth-dimensional, the frequency on Earth fell.

The second reason that Earth fell behind is this: in the third dimension, your solar plexus chakra sends out feelers to watch for danger, and through this psychic centre you also absorb the fears of others. Because Earth is the cosmic solar plexus chakra, our planet is absorbing the fears of the entire universe. We have had to transmute these, and this has held us back.

Because we have lagged behind, we are attracting an extraordinary amount of help from the universe during the birth of the new Golden Age. It is as if the baby being birthed has got stuck and needs extra assistance. Great Illumined Beings, angelic beings and wise ones are focusing their light and energy on Earth now. We can ask them for help to birth the new according to divine timing.

*The 20 years between 2012 and 2032 are unique
in the history of our planet. There has never been
an experience or opportunity like this. You have
incarnated now to help birth a fifth-dimensional
Golden Age in an entirely new cosmic cycle.*

The time-frame

The preparations for the end of one era and the beginning of the next
are similar to those of leaving one house and moving to a bigger one.
Planning, deciding what to throw away and what to take, packing
and organizing the new home all commence well before the move
itself. The timeline for Earth, starting before 2012, is as follows.

1987: The Harmonic Convergence

On 25 August 1987, a planetary alignment activated a 25-year
period of purification to prepare for 2012. In order to facilitate
this, the Violet Flame of Transmutation was returned for our use by
St Germain, working with Archangel Zadkiel.

2012

This year marked the predestined end of an out-breath of God.
This was the conclusion of 10 cycles of cosmic eras, a 260,000-year
period. At 11.11 on 21.12.2012, there was a divine pause, known
as the Cosmic Moment. Source energy touched the heart of every
being on Earth, and on every planet, star or galaxy in this and
every other universe.

In that instant, an in-breath of God was triggered throughout
the cosmos and a 20-year passage to a higher frequency commenced.
Every planet, star and galaxy in this and every other universe
started to ascend to a higher dimension and a new cosmic epoch
was initiated.

At the same moment, 33 cosmic portals throughout the planet carrying Christ Light started to open, radiating high-frequency energies in order to prepare the world for the new Golden Age. Many other portals and pyramids also awoke.

From the Cosmic Moment, this entire universe was given 20 years to clear out anything associated with the lower vibration and embrace the fifth dimension. Because we on Earth were behind-hand, for the reasons I have mentioned, we had only 20 years to make a double-dimensional shift from the third to the fifth dimension. Nothing like this had ever happened before, and a concentrated programme began!

2017

In 2017, the cleansing of the planet was stepped up. It was decreed that this would be done by the elements, so flooding, earthquakes, hurricanes and wildfires intensified for five years. This was to clear the pockets of negativity, free the ley lines and dissolve the karma that had been preventing us from connecting with the pure vitality of Earth.

2022

This was the last year of major purification, so the incidences of extreme action by the elements should calm down now. The Turkey–Syria earthquake in early 2023 is destined to be the last devastating earthquake. The old third-dimensional paradigm will finally collapse and, despite quite a bit of chaos, a more optimistic feeling will spread. We are to start drawing up clean energy, as well as the love of Lady Gaia, through the soles of our feet as we walk. This will massively change how we feel.

In 2022, a period of controlling Saturn's dominance ended and the more bountiful and expansive Jupiter became more influential.

As citizens everywhere realized how we had been manipulated, people power and mass unrest started to change the balance of control on the planet.

2023–2032

Between 2023 and 2032 the world will start to look towards the new Golden Age. Fresh ideas and plans will be put into place by the people for the people.

> *In 2032 a new blueprint will be activated for the entire universe that will enable the next Golden Age to reach an even higher frequency than the Golden Age of Atlantis.*

The population of Earth

The optimum population of Earth is 2 billion. Currently there are 8 billion. There is a spiritual reason for this mass influx of souls. Because this is the end of a 260,000-year cosmic period, Source granted a dispensation to allow all those with karma outstanding to return now to try to complete it.

Millions of souls with heavy karmic debts to repay have taken advantage of this opportunity. However, when we enter Earth and go through the Veil of Amnesia, we forget our origins and divine connection. We also forget our soul contract and life mission. Many of those who have returned to try to atone for their previous misdeeds have forgotten this and are now causing problems as they fall back into their old ways.

At the same time, millions of lightworkers have incarnated in order to birth the awesome Golden Age.

The aim of every lightworker is to help
as many people as possible to ascend to
the light during this crucial period.

Gaia will be fully fifth-dimensional by 2032, regardless of people's decisions and actions. People who have not awakened spiritually and opened their hearts by that date will choose to return to the inner planes or move to another third-dimensional plane where they can continue to experience drama. There will be a big decline in population.

The children incarnating for the new Golden Age will be of a much higher frequency, ready to take our planet to previously unexplored heights.

VISUALIZATION TO LIVE IN THE GOLDEN FUTURE

- Take a moment to relax.

- Imagine a world where everybody is happy and healthy.

- Everyone is contented because they are fulfilled at a soul level.

- People everywhere co-operate and look after one another.

- There is enough for everyone.

- We all respect one another's race and religion.

- The land itself is pure and shining.

- Every day we draw in clean energy from Earth and breathe pure air.

- This is the new Golden Age into which we are moving.

- How does it feel to live like this?

Chapter 3

What Is Happening Right Now on Earth?

Have you ever had a new kitchen installed? If so, you may remember the feeling when all the old cupboards are being knocked out and there is dust and dirt everywhere. And because the new kitchen will be much bigger than the old one, walls are also being demolished as the expansion takes place. You may be wondering why you are putting yourself through all this!

But then you think about the beautiful kitchen that is coming and this gives you the energy and impetus to go on. Soon you will have an amazing shiny, spacious, brand-new one. It will be so much better than the old one. When it is in place, you may wonder how you could have lived with the outdated kitchen for so long.

While it only takes weeks to plan and install a new kitchen, it takes years for Earth to move from a third-dimensional to a fifth-dimensional paradigm, and of course the demolition of a way of life and the building of a new world present challenges. The entrenched forces do not want change. They sense the inexorable rise in frequency on the planet now, for the light is getting brighter all the time, so they are trying to tighten their grip, and this is causing disruption. As soon as the frequency of humanity is higher than that of the current situation, though, the chaos and control must dissolve.

Lightworkers are being asked to hold the vision of the new and keep their lights blazing, no matter what.

Covid

It is interesting that the pandemic was expected by most of the governments in the world. Plans were put into place, but were not actioned. Spiritually, this was because the world needed Covid as an accelerant to move beyond the old ways. The pandemic created the worldwide chaos and disruption that are accelerating the collapse of the old paradigm. Before it was unleashed, I was wondering how the forecasts for changes in travel, education, government, business, economics, banking, health, farming, etc. could possibly happen by 2032. Then suddenly they were all happening rapidly. It wasn't just the physical world that was transforming either – human awakening was occurring in front of our eyes.

My friend Tim Whild had a nasty bout of the virus. He told me that his experience caused him to tune in to and talk to the Covid virus entity. He was expecting a dark being to emerge. Instead, a beautiful pink, white and yellow angel appeared. It told him that viruses come into you to clear out lower vibrations and anything you need to release from your physical, mental, emotional or spiritual bodies.

At a spiritual level, the Delta variant was about clearing the heart chakra. People were literally coughing out old energy. Omicron was often accompanied by splitting headaches that were clearing the mental body. Each time someone says, 'Omicron,' they are starting with 'Om', calling in Source or the universe, then saying, 'I' or 'self', followed by 'cron'. 'Cron' is derived from the old word for the crown, and Divine Feminine wisdom comes from the crown. So each time you think of Omicron, or verbalize it, you call Source energy into yourself to enhance your Divine Feminine wisdom.

Covid has a higher purpose. It is part of the
plan to raise the frequency on Earth. The
pandemic caused millions of souls to wake up.

Thousands of people died during the pandemic. In a final act of service work, nearly all of these souls chose to take some of the stuck energy of the old paradigm with them in order to clear it from the energy fields of Earth.

Not everyone sees it this way, but many years ago my guide Kumeka told me to give no energy to conspiracy theories, as they came from a dark base. It didn't matter if they were true or not. Currently, disinformation, conspiracy theories, lies and questionable behaviours are widespread. They deflect us all from the true path.

Focus on the new and wonderful
that is soon to be our reality.

By 2022, we were all being forced to pay attention to our gut feelings. Previously trusted corporations and organizations were no longer credible.

We now have to trust our intuition.

What is the new fifth-dimensional blueprint for Earth?

There is a vast difference between the old world and the new one we are creating. It is not just this planet either. Every star and planet in this universe is going through an upgrade to a higher dimension. Lightworkers have incarnated to assist this process of transformation for the entire universe. It is important to help build a high-frequency communication network between Earth and all the stars, planets and galaxies in this universe. This cannot be done without the assistance of humans. It is a major piece of cosmic service work.

In 2032 a new fifth-dimensional blueprint will be put into place for this planet and this universe.

Up to now we have been collectively living in a small scruffy third-dimensional house. However, the house is being demolished around our ears so that a gracious fifth-dimensional mansion can start to be built in 2032. The demolition process will continue until 2023. Then we have nine years to get the site ready for the building work to commence. During that period we have the opportunity to study the architect's plans and prepare appropriately.

The best way to clear the site and order the building materials (prepare for the new blueprint) is to live in a fifth-dimensional way. Every fifth-dimensional thought, word or action is creating a building brick for the future. Then as soon as the planetary energy is right, the new can easily come into manifestation.

Planning permission has already been granted by the Intergalactic Council for this next stage of Earth's development.

Just as your personal foundation for your fifth-dimensional self is your Earth Star chakra, so the underpinning for the future is the collective Earth Star chakra of humanity. When enough people have anchored and opened theirs, the basis will be there for the fifth-dimensional golden future. This will take time, but you can help with this visualization:

VISUALIZATION FOR THE FIFTH-DIMENSIONAL BLUEPRINT FOR EARTH

- Take a moment to relax.

- Imagine you are living in peace and harmony.

- You are expressing your creativity and feel great soul satisfaction.

- You are acting as a beacon of light for the world.

- You are remembering your divine essence and connection.

- You are living in a small community with your soul family.

- Everything is grown locally and all your needs are met.

- Everyone is honest and trusting, so everyone shares freely.

- You care for one another within the community.

- New children are being born with their 12 strands of DNA connected and active.

- Everyone has their 12 chakras in place and these are being activated.

- Sense your body moving from a carbon-based one to a healthy, vital, crystalline one.

- The fifth-dimensional blueprint for Earth is bringing Heaven to Earth.

Chapter 4

Negotiating the Path to 2032

The redundant third-dimensional paradigm on Earth is now being swept away. The old economic, health, education, business and financial structures that do not serve the highest good are being upgraded.

Humanity is starting to demand fairness again.

More and more people are bringing in their fifth-dimensional chakras, and this will dramatically change everything. For example, as the navel chakra of humanity opens, people everywhere will seek equality and oneness. Individuals everywhere will reclaim their own authority. As a result, people power will sweep away entrenched regimes, systems and *modi operandi*. That is what happens when just one of the 12 chakras is established.

Energetic rebalancing

We are now seeing the return of feminine energy. Out-of-control masculine energy without the balancing wisdom and nurturing of the feminine is dangerous. Feminine without the strength of the masculine is ineffective. We need a balance.

We have just experienced 10,000 years of masculine governance. How did this come about? The Cosmic Era of Atlantis was to last for 260,000 years, during which five experiments were tried and failed. When the continent was submerged for the fifth and last time, 10,000 years of the era remained. The Intergalactic Council proposed a new experiment for Earth. What would happen if masculine energy prevailed?

Males agreed to take on a dominant role and females surrendered their power. The result has been the third-dimensional experience we have endured. It has affected life at every level – family relationships, contentment, education, society, health, business, peace, everything.

But now the old experiment is running out of time. All over the world women are beginning to stand in their power, though in many places the old ways have become entrenched and it will take more upheaval to bring balance.

Nevertheless, by 2032 masculine and feminine
will support and complement each other
again. The result will be peace, contentment,
a feeling of safety, the blossoming of love and
everyone working for the common benefit.

An exact analogy is that of perfectly balanced, wise parents. Imagine you have a mother who feels safe and loved and consequently is always loving, nurturing, caring and supportive. She sees your beauty and your best qualities, and constantly reminds you of them. She trusts her intuition.

And your father is loving, strong, protective, proud of you, supportive, reliable and logical. Together they take sensible, wise and positive decisions.

No one has had these perfect parents. However, we can start to construct them internally. We can listen to their voices and act on their wise guidance. The more of us who can create wise inner parents, the more easily we can pass through the transition to the golden future.

With wise inner parents, your inner child feels balanced, safe and loved. This is the energy of the future.

Economic rebalancing

The navel chakra of oneness

During the Golden Era of Atlantis, everyone's navel chakra radiated bright orange with the qualities of oneness, co-operation and action for the benefit of all. This fifth-dimensional chakra was withdrawn at the fall of Atlantis, as it was not viable in a third-dimensional consciousness. Now, as more people once again anchor and activate their navel chakras, businesses structured on a pyramid basis will automatically collapse. We are already beginning to see the inevitable decline of banks, insurance companies, supermarkets and chain stores to make way for the new and so much better.

The navel chakra holds codes of oneness and the higher Divine Masculine energy of strength, fair action, logic and decisions for the highest good. At the same time, it is being balanced by the Divine Feminine of higher wisdom, compassion and love. This means that as we progress towards 2032, there will automatically be a worldwide move towards even-handedness. Decisions will start to be made that support equality and togetherness. People are already questioning the integrity of buying cheap clothes made in sweatshops, or fruit that has travelled halfway round the world. These business practices will cease completely before 2032. As a result, countries whose economies are based on exports will have to be flexible and work caringly to support their populations.

Bringing forward the new economic structure

The mass wake-up of humanity will ensure that the world soon comes into economic balance. We are moving inexorably towards a different financial structure, where there will be equality and abundance for all.

A number of things are contributing to clearing the old and bringing forward the new so that it is in place for 2032:

- The rising frequency is touching hearts and minds and starting to flatten the pyramid of inequality.

- More and more courageous souls, from whistle-blowers to truth-seekers, are actively exposing flawed practices, often at a great cost to themselves.

- As the veils are being drawn back on currently accepted economic practices, shocked citizens are demanding a higher quality of leadership. Soon, when the consciousness of the planet is right, people of integrity will step forward to lead by example and inspiration. After 2032, there will be no leaders, as everyone will claim personal authority. In the new matrix, with no ego and a desire to contribute to the highest good, this will be possible.

- The rising consciousness means that the massive divide between rich and poor is no longer being tolerated and there will be widespread protests. Influenced by expansive Jupiter, the masses are already marching in many countries for freedom and fairness.

- Alternative forms of currency will ebb and flow, but these too will pass before the new Golden Age.

- The biggest factor contributing to change is that the economies of countries throughout the world are starting to collapse. The cost of fuel and the ecological impact of transporting goods around the world are biting into international trade, which will soon no longer be viable or morally acceptable. This will massively affect our current way of life and we will pass through a period of hardship unless we work together.

Already, community hubs, sharing schemes,
co-operatives and alternative ways of living
are proliferating. These grassroots economic
movements will grow and spread.

The more that communities and countries
come together and make choices for the
highest good of all, rich and poor alike, the
easier the economic transition will be.

The next step

As the economic structures we have relied on for 10,000 years are swept away by the rising vibration, individuals, communities and countries will have to become self-sufficient. For some, this will be a struggle, but as communities work together for the common benefit, this step will bring us all together.

For anyone whose ego is invested in material goods, the shifts will be a challenge, while those whose satisfaction comes from nature or service will flow with the changes.

Increasingly, commodities will be bartered, shared or freely given. Already there is a rise in charity shops, markets and swap schemes.

Co-operatives and self-help groups will flourish.

Eventually, the tide of the new consciousness will sweep the old economic structure away completely.

Insurance

Insurance companies are being dramatically hit by the cleansing of the planet by fires, earthquakes, volcanoes, hurricanes, floods and unexpected disasters. When these companies can no longer survive, we will have to rely on one another for help in times of need. Support schemes will be set up, and this will engender a feeling of community and safety as we all help one another.

In the new Golden Age, the consciousness will be totally different. Supporting one another, trusting the universe and knowing that our needs will be met will enable us to move into an utterly different scenario where insurance is unimaginable and not needed.

Peace

Because the frequency of humanity is inexorably rising, we will be moving towards world peace by 2032. Each time you choose a peaceful response over a belligerent one, you are helping to bring it forward. We can all make a difference.

Higher than Atlantis

The new Golden Age will be a higher vibration than Golden Atlantis, because the Atlanteans achieved fifth-dimensional consciousness while the planet itself was third-dimensional. In our golden future we will experience fifth-dimensional consciousness supported by a fifth-dimensional planet. Our gifts, powers and achievements will be beyond our wildest imaginings. Yet we are inevitably moving towards this. The new Golden Age is written in stone. It must arise.

VISUALIZATION FOR THE TIME WHEN
YOU HAVE POWERS AND GIFTS

- Take a moment to relax.

- Picture a world where men and women honour, respect and support each other. Everyone acts for the highest good and from the deepest wisdom.

- Imagine you have great powers and gifts and are using them for the common benefit.

- What do you do and how does this feel?

Chapter 5

Cosmic Happenings in 2032

The future after 2032 is inconceivable to our current comprehension. However, some things we can understand. Some are predestined.

When our planet fully ascends to the fifth dimension in 2032, it will propel every human and animal to a higher frequency.

Predestined cosmic happenings in 2032

We access pure love

Hollow Earth is the seventh-dimensional chakra in the centre of our planet. Light flows from the heart of Lady Gaia, the vast angel who resides here, into Glastonbury, the heart chakra of Earth. From there, there is a portal to Venus, the Cosmic Heart that was anchored and activated by Jesus during his lifetime. By 2032, the heart of Lady Gaia, the planetary heart of Glastonbury and Venus will all be in alignment, so there will be a clear channel between them and beyond to Source. This will enable humanity to access a higher quality of love. Every being on Earth will experience the feeling of being loved and belonging. Universal love will touch us.

The planets communicate with one another

Just like Earth, every planet, star and galaxy in this universe has a seventh-dimensional hollow centre, which is its heart centre. By 2032, the heart centres of all the planets and stars will connect and will all start to communicate. This has been an ongoing process that commenced in 2012 at the Cosmic Moment, when the kundalini of Earth started to rise and reconnect us to the stellar world. By 2032 this will enable universal love, peace and heartfelt joy to spread throughout the cosmos.

When this huge cosmic heart opening has been activated, many of us will be able to communicate with beings from other star systems and receive their advanced knowledge as well as their wisdom. While some individuals have been receiving telepathic information and downloads from star beings for some time, this will become generally available. We will start to receive knowledge and wisdom from the stars.

When this has happened, soon after 2032, international peace and co-operation will prevail throughout our planet. This is very important for the cosmic progress of Earth. When it is established, all countries will start to work together for the highest good of all.

The portal of pure love in China opens

When international peace and co-operation signal that Earth and all on her are fifth-dimensional, the Amethyst Skull, which holds the information of the 12 Atlantean clear quartz crystal skulls and is currently dematerialized and held in the inner planes, will start to release its light. (*For more on this, see the following chapter.*)

Simultaneously, a special portal in the beautiful mountains of China containing diamond-white love frequency will start to open. Then the most incredible true and pure love energy will flood our planet and transform us in a way that has never been possible before. By opening the higher hearts of the masses, it will move us all into fifth-dimensional consciousness.

From that time, people everywhere will be able to tune in to the Amethyst Skull and download much sacred information.

All the portals open fully

The 33 cosmic portals bringing in Christ Light started to awaken in 2012. They have been slowly opening ever since. Almost all of them will be fully expanded by 2032 and will be radiating the highest frequency of Christ love, which is pure white. This will bathe everyone on the planet. The more we invoke the Christ Light in the years up to 2032, the more we will be able to absorb at that time.

Millions of portals, crystal grids and sacred stone circles throughout the world were switched on in 2012. Most will be radiating fully by 2032 and will light up everyone in a wide vicinity. At that time, seams of precious gems, the materialized energy of the archangels, will become active, shining out the qualities of their archangel. Imagine living near a mountain containing seams of Archangel Raphael's emeralds, spreading abundance consciousness as well as higher healing! The energy of every spiritual ceremony, ritual or event that has been placed within a crystal will become available. Billions of crystals, small and large, are still waiting to go live and will be broadcasting codes of light.

The Metatron Cube comes together energetically

Earth, Neptune, Sirius, the Pleiades and Orion are all ascending together and are closely connected. These five cosmic entities are symbolically represented in the Universal Metatron Cube and will come together energetically in 2032.

This means that Neptune, Sirius, the Pleiades and Orion will no longer be magnetically pulling us up to their frequency. Instead, we will all be attuned and working together within a globe of pure white Source love.

Unimaginable bounty comes to us

These significant cosmic events will shape the fifth-dimensional future of Earth and will trigger world peace and international co-operation. As soon as this is achieved, Earth will send out a fifth-dimensional energy that attracts massive abundance. This will come to us in many forms.

VISUALIZATION FOR THE WORLD AT PEACE

- Take a moment to picture the entire world at peace and all countries working together.

- Visualize new technology being downloaded so that it can be shared.

- See the world finding new ways of growing food, purifying water and accessing free ecological power from sources that are not yet available.

- Envision us all being able to travel safely at mind-blowing speeds.

- Sense the wonderful happiness, creativity and soul satisfaction of the golden future.

- Imagine the planet surrounded by a golden aura.

Chapter 6

The Influence of the Cosmic Pyramids and Crystal Skulls

Pyramids are computers. The original six cosmic pyramids constructed after the fall of Atlantis are in Greece, Tibet, Mesopotamia, Egypt, Central America and Peru. Those in Mesopotamia, Greece, Tibet and Peru have been destroyed physically, but energetically they are still active. They are programmed with the higher knowledge of the universe. They have also been preset to activate various portals, crystals and the kundalini of the planet, so that we are primed for the golden future.

When Atlantis fell, six of the High Priests and Priestesses took with them the knowledge and wisdom to build these cosmic computers. These were:

- **Apollo**, working with Archangel Michael, who generated the one in Mesopotamia (Iraq). It was programmed to bring the entire cosmos into the harmony of the fifth dimension. Freedom is an essence of harmony, and this pure energy has already stirred those living in the Middle East to liberate themselves and is now spreading its influence across the globe so that people everywhere will be free in the golden future.

*The desire for freedom
is currently stirring mass unrest.*

- **Poseidon**, overseen by Archangel Raphael, created the one in Greece. When it was destroyed by an earthquake, the Parthenon was built on the site. Poseidon had a profound understanding of natural forms of healing, including the mind–body connection. He also had great knowledge about the stars and their influence on the tides and the growth of plants. All this information and wisdom was placed in his pyramid and will ensure that Greece will be a leading force in the return of natural healing.

- **Zeus**, in alignment with Archangel Christiel, oversaw the building of the pyramid in Tibet. His mission was to enable people to enter the silence and spread peace and harmony. This will enable us to develop the qualities of compassion, love and harmlessness. The light from this pyramid in Tibet will touch the hearts of everyone with peace and oneness in the golden future.

- **Thoth**, working with Archangel Michael, created the pyramid in Peru. He was teaching us to understand the proper use of energy, and this knowledge was programmed into the pyramid so that in the golden future we would be able to bring everything into harmony and alignment.

- **Aphrodite**, working with Archangel Chamuel, created the Mayan pyramid in Mexico. As she originated from Venus, her pyramid was coded with pure love and advanced astronomy and mathematics. It holds the keys to enable people to find their self-worth and to truly love themselves by connecting to their divine selves. The energy held in this pyramid is already enabling people to access their divine blueprint and that of the planet. It will help propel everyone into the fifth dimension.

- **Ra**, co-operating with Archangel Metatron, oversaw the building of the pyramid in Egypt. The light from the seventh dimension comes down to Earth in a downward-pointing triangle, while the light from Earth reaches up to the spiritual world in an upward-pointing triangle. Together these create a six-pointed star. This cosmic symbol is anchored into the pyramid in Luxor to bring Earth to Heaven and Heaven to Earth.

The crystal skulls

During the Golden Era, Atlantis was divided into 12 regions, each overseen by a High Priest or Priestess. The original 12 were Thoth, Isis, Horus, Ra, Sett and Imhotep, Hermes, Zeus, Aphrodite, Apollo, Poseidon and Hera.

As the frequency rose, more evolved High Priests and Priestesses were needed, so new ones took their places, but the 12 who had initiated the golden time returned when the experiment was collapsing. Their mission was to lead the survivors to new parts of the world that had been specially prepared.

Thoth, Isis, Horus, Ra, Sett and Imhotep later became Egyptian gods, while Hermes, Zeus, Aphrodite, Apollo, Poseidon and Hera became Greek gods. Each of them used advanced mind control and sound to create an advanced crystal computer to hold all the information and wisdom of their tribe for future civilizations. The decision to create these computers was taken by the High Priests and Priestesses in consultation with the Intergalactic Council. It was the latter who decided that they should be fashioned into the shape and size of a human skull, representing the thought power and consciousness of a human. So these computers are the 12 crystal skulls that are a legacy to help us in the golden future.

For a time, the crystal skulls were housed in the temples of each region, where they were looked after by the priestesses of the temple. The intention was that when a human was sufficiently pure to tune in to a skull, it would allow the connection. It would also send out magnetic pulses to those individuals to stimulate the link! This is starting to happen energetically now.

The Amethyst Skull

Before the final collapse of Atlantis, there was an awesome ceremony. Representatives of the Intergalactic Council attended, as well as representatives of the many Councils of Light. This event was considered to be of such cosmic importance that beings were sent from Lyra, Saturn, Orion, the Pleiades, Sirius, Jupiter, Venus, Andromeda and other stars, planets and galaxies to add their light and their blessings.

Flanked by their temple priests and priestesses, all the High Priests and Priestesses held their own crystal skulls, and during this ceremony all the information from each of the skulls was transferred to a glorious Amethyst Skull, often referred to as the 13th skull.

Just before the flood that engulfed Atlantis, the priestesses took the crystal skulls from their temples and hid them in their new locations.

The Amethyst Skull was placed in the charge of the Sphinx, the pure and powerful guardian of the planet whose energy had been on Earth from the beginning. Originally the Sphinx put a force-field of protection round Earth, but humankind drained its power down to 2 per cent, so that it could no longer fulfil its purpose. As a result, for aeons Earth has been vulnerable to external forces, as is a person with a weak or non-existent aura, but as we become more spiritual, our energy will recharge the Sphinx. Already the force-field has reached 32 per cent of its original strength, but it will not be fully effective until after 2050.

The statue on the Giza plateau represents the energy of the Sphinx. It is connected to Nigellay, the ascended aspect of Mars, the fifth-dimensional peaceful warrior.

The Sphinx will release the Amethyst Skull when all 12 skulls have emerged and our frequency is ready. As the portal of the Sphinx opens, it will massively impact the world with peace energy.

VISUALIZATION TO CONNECT
TO THE AMETHYST SKULL

- Breathe comfortably for a moment.

- Imagine that the world is totally at peace and everyone is radiating a soft golden aura.

- Visualize the Amethyst Skull sitting gloriously between the paws of the Sphinx.

- It is sending out white and gold rays of harmlessness and peace to all parts of the world.

- Then look closer and see that it is radiating rays of harmlessness and peace to every star, planet and galaxy in this universe.

- See or sense the aura of Earth becoming stronger and more golden.

Part II

The Transformation: Life in the New Golden Age

Chapter 7

Living in the Fifth Dimension

In fifth-dimensional consciousness, there is no ego and therefore no personal aspiration or desire to be better than another. When we are not involved in power struggles, drive or ambition, all the energy that has been consumed by proving ourselves is available for creativity, glowing health and the expression of whatever brings us joy. We are happy to use that energy for the greater good of all. As the frequency everywhere rises, more people will naturally feel like this and it will create a wonderful sense of alignment and inner peace.

How much energy would you have available if you had never tried to prove yourself to your parents, your boss, your extended family, your neighbours or, even more important, yourself? Many of us decide that we need to work hard, be competitive and strive to do better in order to earn a living or provide for our family. We believe we need a bigger salary to buy a more spacious house for our children. A huge car is necessary for better holidays. We can always justify driving and striving. But here is the amazing thing:

When your consciousness is fifth-dimensional,
you naturally attract abundance.

Abundance

As humanity becomes fifth-dimensional, we will draw incredible abundance from the universe. This means plenty of nutritious food, technology that supports us, limitless ecological and free power and all that we need.

In the new Golden Age, all the things you have been striving for will come to you naturally if they are for your highest good. And if something isn't for your highest good, why would you want it?

If you rationalize that it is important for your child's future that they attend a prestigious school or have a car, remember this:

> *If something is for your highest good, the*
> *universe will arrange itself so that it is*
> *for the highest good of everyone.*

And the converse is true. If it isn't for your highest good, it isn't for the highest good of anyone else. So, as we move forward, always ask to be guided to do what is right for you.

It is almost inconceivable to us now that the energy of the universe can work so powerfully to support us. However, in the golden future, if you require a bigger home, your dream home will automatically and instantly be provided. If you need to travel somewhere, transport will be there, right outside your door, waiting for you. If it is right for you to have a dog, guess what? The perfect pup will be sitting on your doorstep.

To third-dimensional consciousness, this seems like magic. In the fifth dimension, it is the natural result of energy flowing freely.

The corollary to this is that you do not need to own anything. Why would you want personal belongings if your needs were automatically provided? Why clutter the street up with parked cars when transport arrives as soon as you require it? Why own a home if the perfect house is always available to you? Why own a kite-surfer if one is waiting for you on the beach when you want to fly over the waves?

Ownership is based on the belief that only money will enable you to get what you want. In the new Golden Age, we will all trust that our needs will be provided for. Collective fifth-dimensional consciousness naturally supports this.

When all your physical and emotional needs are met, your spiritual journey becomes more important than personal advancement, and you can relax into a fulfilled life. When your 12 chakras are open, there is deep satisfaction in connecting with Lady Gaia, communing with the angelic realms, downloading information from wise stellar beings or tuning in to the peace of the cosmos. And as you climb to the higher rungs of the fifth-dimensional ladder, even reaching the sixth dimension or touching the seventh, this spiritual journey becomes even more illuminating.

Balance

One of the ways in which the Atlanteans of the Golden Era maintained their high frequency was keeping everything in balance. They always balanced giving and receiving, for example. Nowadays, it is quite common for generous people to give and give. They think that this is earning them spiritual points. In fact, the reverse is true, for giving without reciprocation is considered to be a kind of spiritual control or one-upmanship. It is important to receive so that you allow the other person to experience the joy of giving. It doesn't have to be the same thing. You can bake a cake in exchange for gardening or offer some apples for cleaning. In the golden future, when money is obsolete, there will only be exchange or giving freely with pure love.

*Giving freely with pure love
activates the Law of Grace.*

When our fifth-dimensional heart centres are fully awake, we will be ready to serve one another for the highest good, and this will arise from a deep spring of love within. It will bring a great feeling of satisfaction.

Harmlessness

One of the fifth-dimensional qualities is harmlessness. When you are totally harmless in thought, word and action, every person and creature feels safe with you. Consequently, nothing and no one will hurt you. Animals totally trust you and relax in your presence. As more people's heart centres open and we develop harmlessness, we will once more live in harmony with the animal kingdom.

Humans and animals will live in
amity and mutual respect.

The wonders of the universe

As our fifth-dimensional chakras awaken and reveal our gifts, talents and awesome powers, we effortlessly open up to the wonders of the universe and attune to the spiritual worlds.

Fifth-dimensional people, especially those who were once connected with Lemuria, have a natural love of nature, trees and the land itself. Lemuria was the fourth Golden Age on the planet, the one that preceded Atlantis. Lemurians formed a vast fifth-dimensional healing light force. They were a collective energy that worked through the universe, touching places that needed their energy. Their healing was said to be the purest and most powerful available, for it was completely without ego and sent as a collective energy.

The Lemurians had a deep connection with our planet and loved nature and working with the elementals and dragons. They even drew love and light down from Source through the Cosmic Heart and projected it into Earth.

Many Lemurians have returned now to help us all connect to nature. Indeed, it is very important for the golden future that everyone is at one with the natural world.

Just being in nature enfolds you in a
sense of contentment and aliveness.

You can make a two-way connection by leaving golden footsteps wherever you walk: you channel higher energies down through you into the land and at the same time you bring love up from Lady Gaia's heart. This comes up through your Earth Star chakra below your feet and rises through you to your heart. There it spreads out and touches people, animals and nature.

When you take a conscious fifth-dimensional walk, your light shines very brightly. You can take the following walk in your imagination or find a place in nature and do it physically.

VISUALIZATION TO TAKE A FIFTH-DIMENSIONAL WALK OUT IN NATURE

- Close your eyes and imagine that you are outside on a beautiful sunny day.

- Take a few deep breaths and become aware of the trees and flowers.

- Look at the colours and shapes.

- Smell the scents of the natural world.

- Walk forward and notice how your feet feel each time they connect with the Earth.

- Then imagine the crown of your head opening.

- See or sense golden light pouring down into it and right down through you, then into your feet and the land.

- Know that you are leaving golden footsteps behind you.

- Now, as you breathe in, sense you are drawing up golden light from Lady Gaia's heart.

- Feel it come up through you and breathe it out of your heart.

- See how it is touching the world of nature.

- When you have finished your walk, picture the trail of golden footsteps you have left behind you.

Chapter 8

Economic Metamorphosis

Our attitude to money and business is undergoing a seismic shift! The new Golden Age will see a complete economic metamorphosis.

In the third-dimensional scenario, a pyramid of power results in a detachment between the dominant at the top and the impotent in the lower ranks. There has been a heart and mind disconnect that has enabled banks, economic institutions and big businesses to act in the ways that they have done for so long.

In future, people will find it unbelievable that financial bodies have been allowed to lend illusory money, money that does not actually exist, and charge interest on it in a way that has created hardship and exacerbated the divide between rich and poor throughout the world.

Lending imaginary money has now progressed to selling imaginary property in the metaverse. As the fifth-dimensional blueprint starts to activate within humanity so that abundance consciousness becomes the norm, people will no longer seek wealth in this way.

Businesses that will succeed

In the old world, the universe supported intention, focus and action, regardless of the consequences. That is no longer the case. The universal flow of energy on Earth is changing. As we move towards a higher-frequency world, different criteria will apply.

These are some of the jobs and businesses that will thrive and receive the blessings and support of the universe:

- Jobs and businesses that give soul satisfaction.

- Businesses founded on pure intentions.

- Those that serve people or nature or animals.

- Those that promote good health, perhaps with food or essences, and are authentically in tune with the new age.

- Research that contributes to the genuine welfare or progress of the world, such as nature conservation or free power.

- Businesses based on *heartfelt* creativity, artistic and musical expression.

- Natural healing modalities.

- Co-operatives.

The economy of the new Golden Age

After 2032, money will cease to be relevant.

There will be no money. Everything will be happily shared, exchanged or given away.

New spiritually based technology means that there will be ample for all. Anything surplus to requirements will be pooled so that anyone can freely take it.

In the fifth-dimensional consciousness, humanity will automatically attract abundance and everyone's needs will be met in ways that we cannot currently conceive.

VISUALIZATION FOR THE ABUNDANCE OF THE GOLDEN FUTURE

- Relax as you picture a fifth-dimensional world where there is no ego.

- With self-esteem and confidence, you have nothing to prove.

- You enjoy deep inner contentment, as do those around you.

- There is plenty for all.

- Anything you need automatically comes to you.

- How much are you happy to share?

- How does this feel?

Chapter 9

Education

The spiritual purpose of education is to draw out the soul gifts of a child so that their inner light is illuminated.

In the Golden Era of Atlantis, this is exactly what happened. Priests who were trained psychics would check a child's soul history to understand what their special aptitudes were. As the child grew up, their parents would carefully nurture and develop their talents. But more than that, the child was considered an integral part of the entire community and everyone lovingly helped to develop their abilities.

Every single child was cherished. When they were quite young, children were taken to a nursery each day, where teachers specially chosen for their ability to teach children of that age helped their social development. Priests oversaw their spiritual growth. They were outside in nature as much as possible and learned through play and creativity until they were seven.

From the age of seven, they were taught in the temples. Education was always designed to foster the right brain and to be interesting, enjoyable and fun. Social skills and connection to nature, animals, crystals and the spiritual worlds were given priority.

The memory of these Atlantean teaching methods is encoded within us.

The old matrix

Unfortunately, the current education systems throughout the world are not intended for the highest good of children.

Once the experiment of masculine domination had been implemented, children were generally considered chattels. Few were educated, and those were males only. Rich boys were educated by tutors or went to expensive private schools. Only girls of a high social status were taught anything, and then just a few limited subjects at home.

For a brief period during the Renaissance, however, both girls and boys attended local schools unless they had to earn money for their family. Often students sat on forms facing one another and the older children taught the younger ones. This promoted harmony and respect.

Then the Industrial Revolution came and employers needed a labour force that could read simple instructions and operate machines, so the forms were turned round and children faced the teacher, who stood in front of the class. The children disconnected from one another and this gave rise to separation and its consequences.

For years, teaching has been left brain, consisting of learning by rote or absorbing and regurgitating other people's ideas. For many, it has been boring and frustrating.

Currently, children are massed into huge schools, built to nurse the egos of politicians, that have nothing to do with educating or nourishing the students. The 'one size fits all' system has shut down individuality, creativity and new ideas.

With the rising frequency, many youngsters are now too sensitive to cope with this broken system, and more and more mental health problems are being reported in children and teachers. The seeds of change are sprouting, with more children than ever being home educated.

Lord Kuthumi, the World Teacher, has been working diligently on the inner planes to bring forward a new education system suited to the children of the new Golden Age that will help, encourage and enlighten them.

Education by 2032

The high-frequency children already incarnating are very sensitive and must be treated as individuals. Soon, more children will be born with the slightly elongated heads that house bigger brains. The expanded brains will be configured to understand technology in preparation for the awesome changes ahead.

The new children need creative expression, activity, stimulation, connection to nature and right-brain expansion, and the education system in the new Golden Age will be tailored to their needs.

Schools will be smaller and built locally. These community schools will give a sense of belonging to students and teachers alike.

Teachers will once more be respected and valued. Teaching will be considered an honourable and important profession and only those who are natural-born teachers will be drawn to serve in this way.

Children too will be respected and treasured. These high-vibration children will have come from dimensions where they were honoured and valued. They will know their worth and expect to be esteemed. When they are, they will respond with grace.

Education will be predominantly right brain to promote the flow of creative ideas and imagination. Specially picked and trained teachers will know exactly how to stimulate students and develop their innate gifts. Teachers will understand the influence of harmonious sound to calm, heal, create and balance, so special music, especially angel harmonics, will be played in schools.

Future computers will create pertinent and interesting lessons for students on an individual basis. So, on one hand, there will be more reliance on technology. On the other, children will be taught social skills and encouraged to develop kindness, empathy and integrity. They will practise caring for and nurturing animals as well as connecting to nature. They will learn how to grow food, tend plants and manage their physical bodies with appropriate food, exercise and positive thoughts to maintain optimum health. Fun and enjoyment will be inherent in education.

Sports, especially team games to promote working together and individual excellence, will be supported. Artistic and creative activities of all kinds will be nurtured, especially group activities. Singing and music will be available for everyone and encouraged. Reflecting the high-frequency consciousness of the children, all music will be harmonious, and all students will have the opportunity to learn an instrument if they wish to.

Because every child will be treated as an individual soul, there will be no need for examinations, and these will not be part of the new paradigm. However, those who wish to test themselves in this way can do so.

Children will learn to cleanse energy, work with crystals and develop their psychic skills and gifts. When they are older, further development of their powers, including healing and manifestation, will be wisely managed.

They will naturally connect to the elementals in nature as well as the angelic realms.

Pupils will be taught the spiritual laws, especially the Laws of Gratitude, Grace and Oneness, to keep their frequencies high. Giving thanks will be an integral part of life in the fifth dimension.

The crystalline brain structure

In the new Golden Age, humanity will gradually shift from a carbon to a crystalline base. Crystalline does not infer hardness, like a crystal; rather, people will have the qualities of a crystal. Children will be born with higher-frequency bodies and crystalline brain structures, in which the atoms are arranged according to sacred geometry. The crystalline brain structures will act like neurons, but with advanced connections. They will be sophisticated computers, allowing for massive storage of memory and information, involved calculations, extraordinary creativity and incredible abilities.

*The startling gifts of the new children born
with their 12 strands of DNA connected
and active, and a crystalline brain structure
will be recognized and valued.*

By 2050, both adults and children will be receiving direct downloads of technological knowledge, spiritual information and wisdom from the stars, and this will be honoured and respected.

The crystalline brain will enable everyone to see through the dimensions, so that all can connect to the elementals who look after our natural world as well as to spirits and angelic beings.

VISUALIZATION TO BE A CHILD
OF THE GOLDEN FUTURE

- Imagine you are a child of the golden future with the confidence to do whatever feels right for your soul satisfaction.

- You have a perfect, healthy body.

- All kinds of sports and music are available to you if you want to avail yourself of them.

- You have an incredible brain and can explore whatever subjects interest you.

- Your lessons are specifically tailored to you and they are fascinating and illuminating.

- Every day it is a joy and delight to go to school.

- How does this feel?

Chapter 10

Living in the Golden Communities

We currently cannot have any concept of the peace, joy and soul satisfaction awaiting us in the fifth-dimensional communities of our golden future. It will be unbelievably different from our current way of living. Communities will be much smaller and more contained. People will be totally free to move around and travel anywhere in the world, and will live exactly where they feel they belong. This will happen automatically as the Earth Star chakras of humanity become anchored and activated, drawing everyone magnetically to their divine place of destiny.

People will find themselves with their
soul families and friends.

In the fifth-dimensional abundance consciousness, there will be no need to earn a living. Your living will be divinely provided! So, people will spend their relaxed, leisurely days doing what gives them soul satisfaction. In the old matrix, this may seem boring, but in the new world, the joy of personal expression and service will bring unimaginable harmony, happiness and contentment.

*In the higher consciousness, everyone is totally open,
honest and welcoming. People feel totally safe at all
times. There are no possessions. Why own something
when your heart's desire comes to you automatically?
Everything is freely available. All is shared.*

Leisure

In the last 40 years, the spiritual hierarchy has made more and more technology available. The purpose of this was to give us extra free time to relax and enjoy nature, leisure pursuits and our families. Alas, we did not accept this. We used it to work harder in an effort to make more money and create more things.

This will change in the new Golden Age. With no need to work for survival and with the change in consciousness, citizens will want to spend their leisure hours connecting to nature, expressing themselves creatively and using their physical bodies. Walking, climbing, cycling, exploring and all pursuits that allow them to be outside in the countryside will become increasingly popular.

The golden future is a sociable, fun time. Creativity of all kinds will be enjoyed. Groups will gather to paint, put on plays, make models or pottery, or express themselves in practical ways, both those we understand now and those that are not available to us yet.

*In the fifth-dimensional consciousness of the
golden future, everyone will feel confident and
welcome to participate in any group. Creative
expression of all kinds will be encouraged and
developed in the right way for each soul.*

Sport

Everyone will become taller, thinner and more energetic as we move more into the golden future. Sporting activities of all kinds will be popular, in particular group games. Bats, balls, racquets and clubs will be freely available for anyone to use in sports halls or out in the open. People will be drawn to water sports where the weather permits, for there will be a general understanding of the spiritual qualities and benefits of that medium. Boats of all sorts, from canoes, kayaks and windsurfers to ecologically powered, silent hovercraft will be freely provided, laid out for anyone to use.

In fully established fifth-dimensional consciousness, whatever you need automatically comes to you. So, if you need someone to teach you to sail, that person will arrive. If you need a companion to sail with you, someone on that wavelength will be there. While this is almost incomprehensible to our current way of understanding, that is the energy we are moving into.

Music

Music will be increasingly enjoyed, especially as people comprehend the power and importance of the vibration of sound. Because everyone will be in balance and accord internally, all music will reflect this and be harmonious. Music will be sung and played for relaxation, enjoyment and mood changing. Certain combinations of notes will facilitate manifestation as well as healing.

Musical instruments, both those we have now and new ones to reflect the higher octaves of the Music of the Spheres will be available for anyone who wishes to play them.

People will enjoy forming groups to play their instruments together or gather spontaneously to sing or chant while crowds cluster round to listen.

Everyone will feel welcome to participate at any
time and will have the confidence to do so.

In the higher frequencies, there is regard and care for all things, so equipment is naturally treated with respect. If someone needs to work with a particular instrument or other item, that too is honoured, and it will be returned to the collective pool when it is no longer needed.

Gardening

Gardening will be a popular pastime, and many will enjoy the connection with the Earth and nature as well as the peace that a garden provides. Gardening offers an opportunity for people to communicate with the elementals, especially the fairies and elves.

The great Illumined Master Paul the Venetian is already influencing gardeners to produce many new colours in flowers so, as our consciousness expands, we will be introduced to a wider range of colour frequencies. This will have a subtle effect on us in the same way that music does.

Art

Art has been used throughout the centuries as a way of bringing in rays of high-frequency light. The Renaissance came about because many creative masters agreed to incarnate at the same time with the specific purpose of waking up souls through art. Centuries later, painters like Van Gogh brought in the Christ Light through colour.

In the golden future, the joy of artistic expression will be experienced by the masses. New hues will allow artistically inclined souls to channel and express the higher rays. Artists will often be seen in groups, painting companionably together.

Creative people will express their talents in a number of different ways, some of which we have not yet envisaged.

*Artistic or creative endeavours will all radiate
the intention and channelled energy of their
producers, and when completed, they will
be kept or given away to anyone who needs
that energy or who loves that artwork.*

Celebrations

One of the ways the Atlanteans kept the frequency high in the Golden Era was by enjoying themselves. Everything was celebrated with gatherings – births, birthdays, happy occasions, visitors from another region or simply the impulse to do so. Anything and everything was fêted, and this was a way of giving thanks.

Celebrations cement communities.

VISUALIZATION TO LIVE IN A GOLDEN COMMUNITY

- Take a few moments to relax and close your eyes.

- Picture yourself in a lovely park with a lake.

- There are groups of people everywhere enjoying themselves.

- Some are playing music. Others are singing.

- Athletic ones are participating in sports of all kinds.

- There are groups rambling, climbing, sailing and swimming.

- Others are painting, sketching, throwing pots, sewing and making things.

- You have the feeling of belonging and the confidence to join any of them.

- Whichever group you join, you know you are welcome.

- In your inner world, join a group that interests you.

- Make new friends and try new things.

- Bring the feeling of living in this community consciousness back with you.

Chapter 11

Family Life and Relationships

When the fifth-dimensional sacral and heart chakras are fully established, the cords and lower beliefs that no longer serve people dissolve. Partners and family members attune to each other, chakra to chakra, and especially heart to heart. Because of this, everyone works together for the highest good.

Relationships

In the spiritual world, two people can be unhappily wedded for 40 years and it is not noted as a marriage. Another pair may only be together for a week, but the love is so true and deep that in the Akashic records they are recorded as being a couple.

Marriage is an official human construct. In the golden future, couples will bond for life because they have a true love connection.

> *By 2050, both men and women will only be*
> *interested in relationships that empower them*
> *and enrich them, that enhance their positive*
> *qualities and are based on true love.*

By then, everyone has a sense of self-worth and confidence and respects and honours everyone else. All relationships are based on esteem, honesty and open-hearted acceptance.

Sexuality

It is not by chance that the LGBTQ+ movement is expanding now, for sexuality as we have known it for 10,000 years is starting to become more fluid. As the masculine and feminine energies come into balance and gender-specific roles dissolve, so too do sexual stereotypes. Everyone is free to express their true inclinations. At a fifth-dimension level, sex is an expression of true love.

As we progress into more elevated frequencies, couples will experience transcendent love through sexuality. Increasingly, people will become androgynous, as their own masculine and feminine energies come into balance. Eventually, after 2050, couples will only have sex with the intention of procreation.

Family life

In the golden future, family life will be considered increasingly important. With no ancestral, family or personal karma, children will be born into their soul groups, with parents, siblings and relatives on their wavelength.

Family members will be psychically and spiritually linked to each other. They will understand one another and be telepathically connected and empathically attuned.

In the heart-centred consciousness of the golden future, extended families will be warm, loving, caring and supportive.

Gender roles

For hundreds of years, male and female roles were rigidly understood and enforced, often causing great frustration. But when women started to empower themselves, many took on too much, trying to do everything – earn a living, look after the home and children, and be the perfect wife. Confusion has now arisen in many families about the responsibilities and tasks that each parent should undertake.

At a fifth-dimensional level, parents are regarded as equal but with different roles. Both recognize and accept that they undertook to be male or female for a specific learning experience.

With true love between them, the leisure in which to express their soul desires, and family and community support, life for parents will be unbelievably different from now. It will be joyous and fulfilling.

The spiritual responsibility of a child

Parenting a child is considered to be one of the greatest spiritual responsibilities it is possible to undertake during an incarnation. As couples become aware of just how important a parental role is, they will make their choices with great care.

Singles and those without children

Nowadays many who are single or childless, from choice or otherwise, do not realize that this is a decision taken by their souls.

In the golden future, as now, not everyone will choose partnership or children as part of their life plan. However, they will all feel that they are a beloved and integral part of their extended family and community and will find contentment and soul satisfaction.

In the golden future, people will be aware of their pre-life decisions and will graciously accept their destiny.

Conception

Opportunistic souls, those who seize any chance of an incarnation, will be a thing of the past. In addition, souls will no longer enter challenging families because they have karma to complete. They will be born without karma, so it will no longer influence the decision, and they will choose their potential parents extremely carefully.

Currently, the incoming soul chooses its gender and this will continue to be the case.

Birth choices will be based on the true compatibility
of the incoming soul with their parents-
to-be and the community they will enrich.
A baby will belong to the extended family.

When a couple feels ready to parent a child, the entire family will meet. They will all link heart to heart to discuss with pure intention what kind of soul they can best serve. Naturally the parents will be central to this, for they will have the responsibility for the immediate physical, emotional, mental and spiritual care of the child.

When a decision has been made about the kind of child they can best serve, the couple will connect sexually so that one such soul can be magnetically drawn to them and physical conception take place.

Babies and children

Because they were conceived and born in true love into high-frequency, loving families, babies and children will feel safe and secure. They will be able to open up to their true potential.

Family life will be calm, happy and mutually empowering for everyone.

VISUALIZATION TO LIVE WITH CONTENTED RELATIONSHIPS

- Take a moment to relax.

- Imagine that you are living with your soul family.

- They may be your actual kin or you may choose to conjure up the relations you wish to have.

- Within your family, you are loved, honoured, respected and empowered.

- You are encouraged to be free and express yourself in a way that is right for you.

- You love, honour, respect and empower your family and encourage them.

- Sense how you are connected heart to heart.

- Be aware that you communicate telepathically. Experience how this feels.

- If you are LGBTQ+ or uncertain of your orientation, imagine a soul family in which you are loved, honoured, respected, empowered and encouraged to be free and express yourself in a way that lights you up.

- Enjoy the feeling of belonging and being understood and accepted exactly as you are.

Chapter 12

Home Life

In the golden future, people are in tune with the rhythms of their bodies and the Sun and Moon. Everyone wakes feeling refreshed, because with a relaxed and fulfilling life, good food and healthy exercise, they sleep deeply every night.

Starting the day

The first thing is to give thanks for the new day. Gratitude and attunement to the divine are as natural as breathing to golden people.

The usual pattern is then to enjoy a healthy family breakfast with your soul family.

Off to school

Most children, even young ones, walk to school locally or travel on an individual hover plate. They are totally safe. All forms of transport have sonar that ensures there are no accidents. Travelling to school is a fun experience, for the children are free to run or play or to race each other on their hover plates.

Because parents are connected by a telepathic love link to their children, they don't worry about them or vice versa. Only positive vibrations flow between and around them. All children look forward to school, for it is geared to them individually.

In the home

Within the home, new spiritual technology ensures that everything is easy, automatic and labour-free. Advanced robots are able to do almost anything. You may program one to clean your home or chop vegetables. However, the golden future is about connection, community and service, so if you wish to join others to chat as you prepare food together, then that is what you will do.

Without the need to work as we experience
it now, and no chores or shopping to do,
there is ample time to invest in family life,
hobbies, exercise, fun and the home.

Children and teenagers are always free and welcome to join in any activities, and the consciousness is such that they feel happy to do so.

Because everyone is harmonically attuned, the entire family will want the same thing at the same time.

Crystals

In the golden future, your home is gridded with crystals to hold the frequency high and pure. They are programmed to switch on lights or power or purify the water.

As the era progresses, you will be able to focus the power of your thoughts into crystals to keep the rooms at a perfect temperature and perfectly lit or to switch on beautiful music.

Water

Pure water has cosmic qualities. One of these is the ability to transmute lower energies. Blessed water can dissolve karma. It carries Christ Light, and inevitably, the higher the frequency of the water, the purer the love it spreads. It energizes people and animals who are near it.

As the true properties of water become fully understood, most homes will have a water feature.

Clothes

Almost unimaginable ecological, light, breathable, plant-based materials are available for clothing. They keep you at the perfect temperature and are rain- and windproof. They are also self-cleaning, naturally non-iron and available in a radiant array of gorgeous colours.

Because people are beyond ego, fashion is simply not important, so comfort becomes the only criterion. Most women and many men choose easy-to-wear all-in-one outfits like catsuits.

Alternatively, women may wish to express their femininity by wearing pretty dresses in beautiful materials and glorious colours.

Men will wear whatever is comfortable, whether this be a robe, trousers or a catsuit. Everything will be accepted.

By 2050, as the frequency continues to rise, everyone will be healed of the effects of past repression and will simply wear whatever is most comfortable.

Shoes

The new materials will offer footwear that is incredibly comfortable, breathable, springy and easy to wear. Almost everyone, male or female, will choose flat and comfortable shoes that will enable them to connect to Earth and their Earth Star chakra.

Hair

For ease and comfort, most men and women will choose to have long hair tied back.

VISUALIZATION FOR A DAY IN THE GOLDEN FUTURE

- Find a place where you can be quiet and undisturbed.

- Breathe comfortably.

- And now imagine that you are wearing really comfortable colourful clothing and shoes.

- Look round your home and see the beautiful crystals gridding every room.

- Enjoy the good feeling of knowing that you can program the crystals to provide the perfect temperature and whatever lighting you need.

- Relax and give the robots orders to do what needs to be done.

- Use your time to do what you enjoy.

- Be aware of children going to school on their hover plates.

- Remember when you were a child and could travel on your own hover plate, directing it to your desired destination with your mind.

- Re-experience the exhilaration of racing with your friends.

- And the safe feeling of being able to communicate telepathically with your parents.

- Take a moment to enjoy the feeling of being happy, contented, loved and safe.

Chapter 13

Health and Healing Centres

The current healthcare systems everywhere are collapsing for a number of reasons, mainly because both allopathic medicine and vast, impersonal, specialized hospitals belong to the old age.

In the golden future, hospitals will not be needed. They will be replaced by small local healing centres. Already people are creating health hubs as a stepping stone towards the new.

In the golden future, people will be able to maintain perfect health and equilibrium using natural healing methods. They will visit their local healing temple to be balanced if necessary, or if they need medical assistance after an accident.

The impact of karma on health

During the last 10,000 years since the fall of Atlantis, almost everyone has created karma. Babies have been incarnating with family, ancestral and country karma, not just that of their own soul. For some, this has resulted in deeply entrenched imbalances, dis-eases and mental problems. It is the main spiritual source of syndromes and genetic illnesses, though some brave or generous souls have undertaken these challenges in order to learn a lesson or offer one to others.

The creation of allopathic medicine

As karma piled up, illnesses became more intense and could no longer be healed with natural forms of healing and balancing. This is why allopathic medicines were needed.

Many allopathic drugs have been designed for immediate relief, regardless of side-effects or long-term implications. Old-paradigm pharmaceuticals were a perfect business strategy, where the more you give, the more is needed. However, they are starting to lose their influence because the frequency of humanity is rising rapidly, so natural forms of healing are becoming effective again. They are rapidly regaining credibility and popularity.

Clearing karma

As the old age is closing, all karma has to be cleared. Debts must be repaid. It has always been the case that when parents die, any karmic debt remaining for either of them is shared out amongst the children or grandchildren. If someone dies without children, their cousins or nieces and nephews take it on. However, until recently a soul could decline to undertake this extra burden, in which case that debt would be passed on for up to seven generations. There is now no longer an opt-out clause, so if your ancestors created karma that has not been repaid, it must be borne by you and your siblings or cousins. If you are an only child, you may have to carry it all. That is your soul choice.

Health in the golden future

In the new Golden Age, vibrant health will be valued and people will take responsibility for their own body and wellbeing. For example, if someone has a pain, rather than taking a painkiller, they will tune in to their body to seek the source of the problem, then take natural remedial action.

Holistic health will be taken for granted. Everyone will understand that spiritual, mental and emotional imbalances finally create something physical, so all aspects will be explored and brought into equilibrium.

In the golden future, soil will be restored to
nutritional richness, and fruit and vegetables will
all be organically grown and filled with vitality.
This will dramatically improve health. Drinking
water will be pure and charged with crystal power.

As the frequency rises, all household products, perfumes, sprays and just about everything will contain only natural ingredients that will enhance health and wellbeing.

After 2032, when free eco-power is available, we will breathe pure clean air again. Adults and children will learn to breathe properly in order to relax, oxygenate their cells and revitalize their bodies.

With the decline in population, there will be more space and greenery. As we truly understand just how much nature heals and restores us, trees will be planted and wildflower meadows recreated. In the golden future when people will not need to work for a living, they will enjoy wandering in the green countryside.

With a relaxed lifestyle, plenty of fresh air and
exercise, nourishing light food and happiness, everyone
will maintain maximum health and vitality.

Also, with a feeling of deep contentment, self-worth and belonging, people will not look to drugs, alcohol or stimulants to alter their states. They will simply not be needed.

Transplants

You build your organs with your thoughts, beliefs and emotions, so they contain your consciousness. In order to receive someone's body part, you must have a soul agreement. If you do not, either it will be rejected or a low-vibrational contract will be created. In either case, you have to deal with the donor's energy inside you.

As the new Golden Age progresses, transplants will be almost unheard of. There will be a much greater understanding that life on Earth is just a short experience on a long journey, so people will not be so attached to staying at all costs. There will also be more understanding about letting loved ones go to experience their next adventure in other dimensions.

Local healing centres

Small friendly healing centres to serve the local community will be built in natural surroundings wherever possible. The healing qualities of flowers will be recognized, so beautiful blooms will fill the gardens and fresh ones will raise the vibration in the rooms. Special healing music will be played and soothing colours grace the walls. The sacred qualities of water will also be acknowledged, so healing centres will feature fountains and streams. Crystals will be gridded around the centre.

Those people whose soul mission is to heal will serve in these beautiful healing centres.

Healers will balance people's chakras with
sound, light and spiritual healing to raise them
into the high frequencies of perfect health.

If someone has had an accident, they will lie on a floating oval-shaped disc-bed while healers tend to them. Using plant wisdom, carers will offer herbal concoctions for shock. They will utilize laser lights to knit bones in a way that is currently inconceivable.

For more serious injuries like spinal fractures, a group of healers, usually three, will surround the patient. Together, they will focus sound, thought power and intention onto the patient and use lasers to repair them.

By 2050, people will be able to self-heal and maintain perfect health.

Soon after 2050, people will be able to regenerate limbs. There will also be rejuvenation chambers to revitalize the cells.

VISUALIZATION FOR PERFECT HEALTH

- Close your eyes and breathe comfortably.

- In your inner world, you are happy, positive and healthy, full of life-force and vitality.

- Whatever your age, you can exercise and are agile.

- Your body feels light and free.

- If you have a health challenge, you can self-heal.

- See and feel the revitalized you.

- Bring that feeling back into your day.

Chapter 14

Nature and Food

Soon after 2032, there will be new ways of growing plentiful highly nutritional food.

As international trade diminishes and then ceases, we will eat locally grown or produced food that nourishes our bodies in an optimum way.

Our planet is extraordinary in that every
plant and tree is specifically attuned to nourish
or heal in a perfect way the people that are
indigenous to the place where it grows.

Because everyone will be born into their soul family in their country of optimum happiness, apart from holidays and adventures, people will want to remain where they are attuned to the food they need.

In the golden future, food will be organic, natural and pure, in alignment with the higher consciousness. Monocultures will be replaced by bio-diverse farming. Agroforestry, permaculture, biodynamic methods and other natural organic forms of food growth will flourish. This is already happening in some places. So too is the planting of small community orchards for everyone to share.

As the frequency becomes fifth-dimensional, we will automatically start to eat lighter food grown in rich, nourishing soil.

Food choices

By 2032, most people will be vegetarian, though some will eat fish.

By 2050, many people will be vegan, and the current worldwide move towards plant-based eating is in tune with this.

Those who are at the upper levels of the fifth dimension will live more and more on *prana*, though they will not be breatharians, for that only becomes truly possible for long periods when you are sixth-dimensional.

Quan Yin, the great High Priestess of Atlantis, who later became a goddess in China, was said to live for 2,000 years. She did so by maintaining a fifth-dimensional physical body, during which time she ate very lightly and purely, then rose for a while into the sixth dimension, where she lived on *prana* and was able to regenerate before she returned to her fifth-dimensional physical body.

Breatharianism is not part of the golden future because we are moving into a time of community, sharing and oneness. This includes preparing food and eating with others. Food brings people together.

Everyone will happily drink pure natural water, energized with crystals. Only life-enhancing nourishment will be consumed.

Abundant food

Soon after 2032, new spiritual technology will revolutionize food growing and provide the entire planet with an abundance of delicious, highly nutritious food. It will be freely available, so you can collect whatever you need or it will be delivered by super drone directly to your door. Shopping will be easy!

Vegetables will be grown in vast polytunnels using advanced hydroponics that we cannot even imagine yet. They will be freely shared in the local community. As there will be plenty, people will only take what they need.

There will, however, continue to be those who love to garden and grow their own.

Furthermore, scientific advancements will find ways to keep food fresh, so that freezing, canning and drying will be obsolete. Later we will be able to produce fresh food throughout the year.

Harmlessness

The fifth-dimensional quality of harmlessness will extend to the plant kingdom. Nothing will be picked unless needed, and people will be grateful for whatever they eat.

Everything in the natural world will become safe. Fungi, berries, leaves and bark will lose their toxicity. Trees, bushes and plants will develop without barbs or stings, and they too will gradually become harmless. By 2050, all of nature will radiate a golden aura.

Working with the elemental kingdom

As we raise our frequency, technology will advance and our spiritual and psychic abilities also develop. Soon after 2032, we will generally be clairvoyant and able to see through the veils into the dimension inhabited by the elemental spirits who work with the natural world – the fairies, imps, gnomes, goblins, elves, fauns, salamanders, undines, mermaids and others. We will open up to all that these beautiful beings can teach us about nature, the land and growing food.

These beings are ethereal and invisible to us until we are ready to see them. As spirits of air, earth, water, fire and wood, they are known as elementals because they do not carry all five elements.

You do not have to wait to see these beings to form a relationship with them, though. You can already talk to them with love and respect, trusting that they are listening, and they will respond by helping you.

Air elementals

Air elementals only contain the element air.

The best known and most beloved are the fairies, who tend the flowers and vegetables. They are pure, innocent, playful beings. While some are third-dimensional, many have ascended to the fifth dimension. They are happy to advise us on growing vegetables, so gardeners and food producers will naturally work with them.

When we consciously collaborate with fairies to grow plants, they will deflect harmful insects from eating the crops and encourage beneficial insects.

Sylphs are tiny air spirits who co-operate with the fairies. They keep the air round plants fresh to help them remain healthy and enable the light of the Sun to enter their leaves. They will also work with you to clear your aura or puff away congested thoughts. Air dragons are even more forceful in blowing unwanted energies out of your space and transmuting them!

As yet little known are the esaks, who have only recently been invited to Earth from another universe to help to cleanse the planet. They are vacuuming up lower energies to prepare for the higher frequencies coming in.

Earth elementals

These only contain the element earth.

Pixies are tall. They are trouble-shooters helping people with the structure and quality of soil, so they never stay in one place for very long. So, if you wish to improve your soil, mentally call on pixies to help. They will soon be with you and impress on you what it is best to do. They also direct bees to help get flowers pollinated more efficiently.

Elves work with trees, so ask them what to do to help your trees.

Gnomes are tiny and very shy. They work under the earth with the deeper layers of soil and rocks.

Goblins are very wise fifth-dimensional nature beings. They have developed huge heart centres and a great capacity to love, so they can assist you with many things.

You can call on Earth dragons to clear the energy under your home, especially the ley lines.

Water elementals

These beings only contain the element water.

Mermaids look after the flora and fauna of the oceans, lakes and rivers.

Undines keep the waters everywhere flowing.

Kyhils are new to this planet. They are tiny elementals who have come to help cleanse the waters of the world. You can bless them and consciously direct them to areas that need assistance.

Plants thrive in the unconditional love and protection of the Christ Light that water dragons spread in all water, including rain and moisture in the atmosphere.

Fire elementals

These are beings who only contain the element fire.

Salamanders transmute lower energies in fire. They respond to your emotions, so stay calm when lighting a fire or trying to put one out! They fuel wildfires when humans panic.

Fire dragons are more stable and will protect you and your garden with etheric flames. They will also burn up any negativity around you or in a specific place. They will protect the vast polytunnels of the golden future.

Wood elementals

Warburtons are fifth-dimensional tree elementals and very wise beings. They are mostly found in ancient woodland, but their knowledge and wisdom will be particularly helpful when we start to reforest the world.

Combined elementals

Imps are formed of the combined elements of earth, air and water. These tiny elementals are only 2.5 cms (1 inch) tall and they aerate the soil and help seeds grow. If pixies are in the area, they work with them.

Dragons can be solely of earth, air, fire or water, or a combination of any three elements. These wise, open-hearted beings can help you in myriad ways and can become great friends to you.

Fauns contain the elements of earth, air and water. They help to balance the energy of forests through photosynthesis.

Those who are helping with food production
in the golden future will consciously co-operate
with the elemental kingdoms, so that
crops are luscious and nutritious.

To enable fresh food to be provided all year round,
they will also align with the phases of the Moon, as
past wisdom is recognized and honoured once more.

Working with the archangels

Every colour ray is connected to an archangel, as is every vegetable. Peas have white flowers, so Archangel Gabriel, who operates on the white ray, sends energy to them. His joy and clarity are within the vegetable when you eat it. Many runner beans have bright red flowers and the mighty Archangel Metatron adds ascension vibrations to them when you consume them. I always give thanks for Archangel Uriel's power with wisdom when I eat courgettes, which have yellow flowers. Eating vegetables is one way of absorbing heavenly light.

The Illumined Master Paul the Venetian is working with the archangels to extend the colour rays for the new Golden Age. We can already see this in the rose gold and shimmering multi-tinted hues that are so popular. He is collaborating with Archangel Purlimiek, the Angel of Nature, to expand the colours of flowers. This will enable the archangels to bring higher vibrations through the vegetables of the golden future.

VISUALIZATION FOR FOOD PRODUCTION IN THE GOLDEN FUTURE

- Take a moment to relax and breathe comfortably.

- Imagine you are in a polytunnel of the future, vast beyond your current conception.

- Large crystals grid the area.

- Beautiful soft music is playing.

- A pure, clear, sparkling stream tinkles as it flows through the giant polytunnel.

- All the vegetables are healthy, luscious and growing abundantly.

- Brightly coloured lights are darting about among the vegetables.

- You realize these are fairies. Then you are aware of other elementals.

- They are communicating with the gardeners and helping the plants.

- One comes to you. What message does it have for you?

Chapter 15

Animals

Animals originally incarnated to share our planet with us. They arrived from all over the universes and inhabited different continents just as we did. Some of us had a soul affinity with certain species and they with us. Others felt alien.

The divine plan is that we live and learn together with animals. They are right-brain and heart-centred, while we humans predominantly operate from our left brain and mind. Neither is intended to be superior or dominant.

Animals in Atlantis

Throughout the famous Golden Era of Atlantis, animals were honoured and treated with respect. They incarnated to serve us and everything that they offered was received with love and gratitude.

Cows, bulls, horses, goats, pigs and sheep were considered part of the family. Every child had a dog and a rabbit, while cats watched over homes and temples.

All animals were vegetarian, including cats, who had different jaw structures and digestive organs.

When the energy of Atlantis degenerated, certain humans experimented on and cloned animals. Many of those people have incarnated again during these end times and are repeating their previous behaviour. This will cease as the frequency inevitably rises.

The effect of the Cosmic Moment

At the Cosmic Moment in 2012, when Source energy touched the heart of every sentient being, the spiritual progress of animals accelerated. Many started their journey to the fifth dimension, while those who were already at that level ascended into higher frequencies.

Certain animals have now learned all they need from life on Earth and are ready to withdraw. They will become extinct. However, creatures only become extinct on the surface of Earth. Within Hollow Earth, the vast seventh-dimensional chakra in the centre of the planet, they live on in etheric form.

Other species, who were designed for a third-dimensional world and are not ready or inclined to live at a higher frequency, will return to their home planet or chose to move to another plane similar to that of old Earth. New fifth-dimensional animals ready for the new Golden Age will take their place.

Animals in the golden future

All animals, trees, flowers and vegetables are moving inevitably towards a higher frequency and will soon radiate golden auras.

Farm animals

Some animals have contracted to serve humans by offering produce or muscle power. But by 2032, almost everyone will be vegetarian or pescetarian. By 2050, people will just eat plant-based food. Animal farms will be obsolete and many animals will return to their home planet to process their experiences here and take decisions about their future soul journeys.

Abattoirs will naturally close down and the land
beneath and around them will be deep cleansed.

Where farmers really love their animals, some will, however, stay as companions. The new consciousness means that they will be free. People will continue to care for them where necessary, but the concept of ownership of another creature will have dissolved.

Some farm animals may wish to experience life without the support of humans and they will roam the countryside or forests.

Hens, who come from a 10th-dimensional universe and are highly evolved, will range freely, offering eggs and feathers to those who want them. They originally arrived to demonstrate that service with joy is an important part of the ascension journey, and those who decide to remain on Earth for the sheer delight of being in a physical body will continue to spread happiness and love.

Many sheep, from the Pleiades, will remain, grazing freely, healing people and the land, and offering fleece and even milk where wanted.

Pigs, too, came from the Pleiades to spread love and healing both to people and the land. Despite the way we have treated them, they are willing to stay and continue to support us into the golden future.

The wisdom of goats, from Orion, will be recognized and those who love these animals may continue to look after them. Delighted with the love link, these goats will willingly offer their milk to them to be made into cheese or soap. As we respect them, they will in turn honour us by tuning in to what we need as well as their own needs. They will no longer indiscriminately chew up everything in their path!

Not everything is written yet about the future. Cows are beautiful fifth-dimensional beings from Lakumay, the ascended aspect of

Sirius. They carry divine motherly energy, while bulls embody the Divine Masculine. They incarnated into Golden Atlantis, where they were treated with love and respect, both bulls and cows living as part of the family. In return they gave rich nourishing milk, exactly calibrated to the needs of humans. Since the fall, however, they have been so badly mistreated that several years ago they succumbed to mad cow disease and foot-and-mouth disease, and thousands were cremated. At that time their oversoul was in discussion with the Intergalactic Council about whether they should remain as a species, or leave this planet. They agreed to stay, but it is very much in question whether or not they will remain for the duration.

Pets

Many of us have incarnated with our pets many times, just as we have with our children. The universe ensures that each one is with the right family eventually. Just as an adopted child comes to Earth via another mother before reaching the family of soul choice, so a pet might have more than one home before arriving at the right one. But it will get there. Nothing is by chance.

Dogs come from Sirius and are teaching us about unconditional love. They form an unbreakable bond with the humans who love them and this will continue into the golden future. Almost every family will have a dog, and with smaller communities surrounded by nature, there will be more space for them to enjoy life together.

Guinea pigs incarnate from Venus, the Cosmic Heart. They give and receive love and their purpose is to open people's hearts and heal them. They will continue to do so well into the new Golden Age.

Cats

The cat species originates from Orion. All cats are very wise and incredibly psychic. They know everything that is going on. Domestic cats psychically watch over the family and the home, keeping it clear of lower energies. Tigers and lions watch over the planet, holding back and dissolving unwanted external influences. This is incredibly important, and the entire feline kingdom does an amazing job of looking after us and Earth.

As the new Golden Age progresses, animals who need to eat meat will withdraw from the planet. However, cats will continue their soul progress on Earth, so in the new paradigm of harmlessness, they will have to become non-meat eaters. It will take several hundred years to change their digestive structures as well as their jaws. So, in consultation with the Intergalactic Council, it has been decided that a faster transition will be effected, with each new generation of kittens coming a step nearer to the desired outcome.

The vital caretaker role of cats will, however, seamlessly continue.

Insects

Insects are dying at an alarming rate on our planet. However, as we approach the golden future, the frequencies that have decimated many species will no longer be used. New frequencies will operate at a higher level that is harmless to insects, animals and humans.

Only natural organic growing methods will be used, and as the soil, air and water become pure and clear again, insects will proliferate. They, too, are raising their vibration and are losing their stings.

The fifth-dimensional insects – bees, butterflies, ladybirds and ants – will remain on Earth in the golden future, not only working to help the planet, but also continuing to influence us with the sacred codes they carry.

As the consciousness of humanity shifts dramatically with the onset of the new Golden Age, we will respect and be grateful for all that insects do for us.

The benefits of harmlessness

Remember that one of the key qualities of the golden future is harmlessness. Animals will bring through more wisdom from their home planets to ease the path to friendship between all species. All will be at peace.

By 2050, the world will be a totally unrecognizable place of togetherness and trust. Humans and all animals will live together in amity and peace.

VISUALIZATION WITH ANIMALS IN THE GOLDEN FUTURE

- Find a place where you can relax.

- Take a deep breath and open your heart wide.

- You are in a golden community where animals are loved and respected.

- A golden cloak of harmlessness surrounds you.

- A goat comes to you and you stroke it, receiving a burst of love from its heart.

- Chickens cluck and peck freely round you.

- A wolf comes to sit beside you and you pat it happily.

- All animals are safe and so are you.

- Notice how this feels.

Chapter 16

Houses and Golden Cities

The new Golden Age will be an era of community, togetherness, fun, friendliness and harmony. This will be reflected in the houses, which will be built in groups, nestling into the contours of the land. They will have shared facilities, for these will be considered more ecological and less wasteful and will enable each cluster of houses to be self-sufficient. The concept of personal space will recede as togetherness becomes more important, and this is part of the new consciousness. So, for example, people will join one another to chop vegetables, to eat together and simply to be.

With no ownership in the golden future, there are no boundary hedges or fences between properties. In these heart-centred, leisurely times, there are always adults happy to keep an eye on toddlers. Children, dogs, cats and chickens wander freely, for in fifth-dimensional consciousness there is respect for all, and, as we have seen, this extends to animals.

Another element that marks the new golden time is laughter and lightness. So, fun things that are mostly unimaginable to us now will be built into houses. The current equivalent would be a swing from a tree into a pool, a tunnel with a slide down a slope into a bedroom, or a stream that runs through a sitting room – all unsophisticated entertainment.

Construction

In the fifth-dimensional frequencies, there will be no need for planning permission! There will only be a collective desire and intention to create harmony and beauty for the highest good. This is still unimaginable to our current understanding. However, the new consciousness will manifest an extraordinary new world. A united vision of community homes will allow them to be built in a perfect way, to the satisfaction of all.

An analogy would be a group of musicians coming together to express a theme, perhaps joy. They attune heart to heart and hold the vision of joy, so that they automatically play together and produce something beautiful. And the placement of houses, collective buildings and their infrastructure, roads, new woodland, orchards or wildflower meadows will be decided in the same way.

The houses of the future will be constructed from solid, durable plant material that can be extruded into any shape, using technology of which we currently have no concept. The Divine Feminine will be in evidence and all homes and buildings will be round, oval or curved. In the imaginative golden future, many people will design homes with flowing, unusual aesthetic shapes, with shaped windows. Without angles, the energy can flow easily and this keeps the frequency high.

The only exceptions will be pyramids. Many buildings will be formed in this powerful shape, but this will come later, after 2050, when Earth currents can once more be directed to stream through these structures to support crystals at their pinnacles.

As trees, rocks and natural formations are honoured, buildings will easily and respectfully be built to flow round them.

The foundations of buildings will be of not yet invented materials that allow the earth to breathe. This means that the people living in these homes will be able to connect directly with the love, wisdom and joy of Lady Gaia.

Most homes will be single-storey, because people will want to keep their connection with the earth. Ground-level living will be possible because initially the population will decline, so there will be much more land available. Later, currently uninhabitable land, like deserts and areas now covered in ice, will be reclaimed.

Although all buildings will be created to last, when they have served their purpose, they can easily be taken down, as they will be completely biodegradable. They can also be readily extended if more room is required.

The homes will be light and colourful to reflect the happy mood of the people who construct them and live in them. Windows will be made of a new material not yet invented, that can keep rooms light and bright or dimmed, as well as warm or cool as desired.

Homes will be built by the community. So, if you need a house, a group of willing neighbours, friends or strangers who love building homes will happily join together and create one for you, according to the design you envisage.

In the new consciousness, everyone understands
that we are all one. There is no separation
between what you do for yourself or another.

Using the new materials, homes will be swiftly built by a combination of robot technology and loving personal handcrafting. Later, many of the building materials will be precipitated from the unmanifest realms.

As always, because the higher consciousness is harmonious, all buildings will blend with each other and their natural surroundings.

Conservation and waste disposal

Although eco-energy will be freely available soon after 2032, people will honour all that is provided by nature. Every house will be constructed with underground water storage. Advanced solar panels will grace all roofs. New technology will replace all our services, such as sewage or dustbin collection, with methods not yet conceived.

All food is fresh, so there is no requirement for canning or packaging. Fabrics are self-cleaning and do not crease, so washing machines and irons are obsolete. Refrigerators and freezers will only be used in a few parts of the world. Microwaves designed for a third-dimensional vibration will be upgraded to a harmless form, while cookers and ovens will have changed beyond recognition.

Televisions and our current computers may lurk in some forgotten corner of the attic, and be considered weird antiquities.

All of the goods – vehicles, furniture and more – created in our technological age will need to be disposed of. Soon after 2050, awesome new dematerialization techniques will enable such products to be reduced to their atomic form, and unicorns will take the atomic residue into the universe to be disposed of.

The kyhils, tiny elementals from another universe who have come to help us cleanse the oceans and rivers, have been doing a valiant job. However, as the frequency of the world rises, spiritual technology will take over to purify the waters.

Golden cities

Soon after 2032, golden cities will start to arise around the world. Golden cities are ecological communities built for the highest good of all the inhabitants. They will have little relationship to our current concept of cities, partly because they will be gracious and spacious and will be relatively small. All the houses, land and trees will radiate golden auras.

These cities will naturally be built on ley lines, or where they cross. Each of these communities will be connected to a particular planet or star, and in a few cases to more than one. If you originate from that part of the cosmos, you will gravitate towards that city to connect with your soul friends. It will become a portal to your home of origin.

The first of these wonderful cities will be created in the mountains or in places where snow and ice have purified the land. Later, others will arise in special places where the frequency is high, and attractive single-storey houses will be set around trees and natural formations.

Climate change and some alterations in the geographical structure of the world will mean that conditions are different from now. These will be accommodated in the optimum way. For example, in years to come some cities will be built on water, others within mountains or underground. However, the high-frequency energy and joyous consciousness of the citizens will mean that they can enjoy happy, creative, love-filled and soul-satisfying lives wherever they are.

Everything that applies to the clusters of buildings will apply to the golden cities: the buildings will be communally built, on Divine Feminine principles, by generous-hearted people for one another, and there will be no ownership, for that is deemed unnecessary in the fifth dimension.

Every golden city will be constructed around moving water – a natural spring, river, waterfall or ocean. This will be automatically kept clear and pure by crystals and magnets, in order to raise the vibration of the entire area.

The honest, community-minded inhabitants will create parks, streams and lakes within the cities where boats and sports equipment will be left freely available for anyone to use. Halls will be built by volunteers for indoor sports, art or creative studios and social gatherings of all kinds. In the new consciousness, everyone will feel happy, confident and that they belong, so everyone will feel welcome to take part in any activity.

Within each enclave of the city there will be a communal area for togetherness, laughter and sharing.

Some of the early golden cities will be built in Norway, Sweden, Austria, Germany and Greece.

Greece is particularly interesting, as the Parthenon was built on the site of the cosmic pyramid originally constructed by Poseidon, a High Priest of Atlantis, with the assistance of Athena, a High Priestess of Atlantis. Although the pyramid was destroyed centuries ago, the high-frequency energy and information held within the original building lie there dormant, waiting for the Earth's kundalini to be awakened. When this happens, soon after 2032, a golden city will arise, connected to the healing constellation of the Pleiades. Greece will become a world leader in the health and healing methods of the future.

Finland is holding very pure light and is receiving energy directly from the Arctic, which is the Stellar Gateway chakra of Earth. It will not need golden cities, for the whole country will become a golden community.

Somewhat later, golden cities will be created in Russia, Mongolia and many other parts of the world, bringing joy and contentment to the people. There are also countries, such as Finland, where golden cities will not be built, but golden areas will develop. Here, the land and homes will radiate golden fifth-dimensional light and happiness.

VISUALIZATION TO LIVE IN A GOLDEN CITY

- Sit quietly and close your eyes.

- Imagine that everything around you is peaceful and happy.

- You can hear birds singing, soft wind chimes and the sound of melodious laughter.

- You are walking beside a clear, pure, sparkling stream.

- It runs through spacious, gracious, round, low-rise houses.

- There are green lawns, colourful flowers, trees and fountains everywhere.

- The people you see wave to you.

- You notice that they all move in a leisurely, contented way.

- And you see that everything and everyone radiates a soft, golden energy.

Chapter 17

Travel

People have always wanted to see the wonders of the world. This desire is innate in many of us.

Golden Atlantis progressed from a time when they only had basic necessities and walked along tracks to using unimaginably advanced forms of transport. Even in the early days, some people could teleport and use telekinesis to move themselves and materials from one place to another. Eventually, through spiritual technology, they created hover plates on which both children and adults could travel for short distances along the ley lines. These were crafted from metals that are no longer available on our planet. As the era progressed, silent ecological airbuses, ranging in size from small to vast, travelled at different heights along various frequency bands, at unbelievable speeds.

We have repeated the same cycle of learning about transport, though we have not reached anywhere near the capabilities of the Atlanteans. In the new Golden Age, we will massively surpass their achievements.

Before 2032

During the challenging period up to 2032, travel will become more difficult because the fossil fuel we have been using will be in short supply and will become increasingly expensive. Travel, especially by road and air, will decrease until the new eco-power comes in.

Because of this, the international movement of goods will decline until it eventually ceases, and this will bring about the end of supermarkets and shopping centres. Countries that have relied on exports will need to develop local manufacturing and businesses. Without mass imports and exports all over the world, everyone will depend on home-grown food and locally made products for a few years.

Cycling will become a much more popular form of locomotion, for without fuel and with fewer vehicles on the roads, it will be faster and easier than walking. Public transport like buses, trains and ferries will be popular again.

For a short period, it may seem that everything has regressed, but this is just the recovery period after the old paradigm has virtually collapsed and before the new is available. It is also an opportunity for people to share their vehicles communally.

After 2032

Travel options

As soon as new forms of free eco-power become available, people will resume travelling with enthusiasm, for there will soon be safe, fast options on offer. Transports of all kinds will be constructed from as yet unimagined biodegradable plant material.

In the higher consciousness, whatever you need will be available to you.

Each community will have a pool of vehicles, and if you need one, no sooner have you sent out the thought than it appears for you! This seems incredible to our current understanding. Most cars will be driverless, though some people may prefer to have a driver, in which case volunteers will take on this role. The cars will be totally safe, as we finally learn from bats about advanced sonar. All transports will incorporate technology that ensures they avoid contact with one another.

There will be relatively little traffic on the roads, and houses will be built without garages.

Local travel

To travel short distances, many people, especially children and teenagers, will ride on individual hover plates. These will be like large discs on which you can sit or stand, and they will float above the ground, taking you to the destination you designate.

Most people will be able to levitate and teleport, and I will discuss what this really entails in a later chapter.

Small silent helicopters designed for one, two or a family will also be standard. If you need to travel further than your immediate community, one will arrive to take you there.

Distant travel

There will be large, comfortable, quiet air buses in which to travel longer distances at incredible speeds. There will also be a type of air train, where your own small transport will hook up to an engine with many others going to the same place. You will remain in your individual vehicle as you are all carried at speeds beyond our comprehension to your destination. Here your vehicle will unhook so that you are free to continue your journey as you wish.

When peace and international co-operation have been established in the world, passports and all proofs of identity will disappear. When we recognize that we are one, we will all embrace and welcome each other. There will no longer be any need for boundaries. People will be free to travel anywhere in the world.

Travel by water

As we become calmer and more peaceful and our contemplative fifth-dimensional nature comes to the fore, slow sea voyages or river cruises will appeal to many.

After 2050

Eventually ecologically powered planes, aerodynamically shaped like our current rockets, will transport people across the world at speeds as yet beyond belief, but this will not be until 2050 or thereabouts.

Humanity will once more be allowed to explore space, as the consciousness will be one of humility rather than entitlement.

A return to nature

Spiritual technology will progress very quickly and enable us to do awesome things. However, the more we advance, the more we will wish to return to our roots. Recognizing that the more our Earth Star chakras evolve, the higher we can climb spiritually, we will want to connect with Earth and nature.

Walking and cycling will become a choice for travel as well as for recreational sport. Families and groups of friends will enjoy taking trips together to watch or participate in games with other communities or countries. This will be for fun and the achievement of excellence rather than for competition.

Mountain-climbing, exploring and caving will have increased followings as it becomes easier to reach remote places.

Gardening will be a particular favourite, combining connection with Earth and the natural world with the satisfaction of growing plants and communication with the elemental kingdom. And many will enjoy visiting gracious gardens and beauty spots all over the world.

VISUALIZATION FOR TRAVEL IN THE GOLDEN FUTURE

- Sit quietly and close your eyes.

- Think of a local place you would like to visit.

- See yourself walking to your door, where a form of transport awaits you. What is it like?

- Get into or onto it and mentally command it to take you to your desired destination.

- Enjoy the relaxed, quiet and comfortable journey.

- When you arrive, get out and look round at the new golden world.

- Would you like to visit another country? Decide where.

- Instantly transport will be there to take you to a central hub where you enter a huge rocket-shaped conveyance.

- You chat to your fellow travellers.

- In seconds, you have arrived in the country of your choice.

- Get out and take the time to enjoy this place.

- Return home, knowing you can travel anywhere you like freely, quickly and easily.

Chapter 18

The Law

When the fifth and final experiment of Atlantis was seeded, fifth-dimensional beings from all over the universes volunteered for it. None of them had been to Earth, nor had any of them met before, so it was a journey into unknown territory. These strangers were obliged to share and co-operate, and out of this necessity the Golden Era emerged.

At the start of this period, the High Priest Thoth laid down the spiritual laws for the citizens to live by. There was a long and detailed list of the spiritual outcomes of different actions, and everyone honoured and lived by this wisdom.

When Atlantis fell and the world became third-dimensional, we eventually created our current cumbersome legal system. In the future, our health and safety laws will be regarded with derision, while our arbitrary and antiquated legal system will be viewed with compassion.

In the golden future, there will be no legal system, for it will not be required.

Spiritual laws

When the great Illumined Master Jesus incarnated, he simplified Thoth's spiritual laws into 33 laws plus three transcendent ones. These spiritual laws were divided into four types.

The basic laws of life

'As above, so below' and 'As within, so without' are basic laws. Jesus outlined other basic laws too:

- **The Law of Request**, which reminds you that if you want something from the spiritual realms, you must ask for it.

- **The Law of Attraction**, according to which you attract people and situations that exactly reflect an aspect of you.

- **The Law of Reflection**, whereby every single thing that happens in your life reflects something about you, so for example if you bump your car, ask yourself who or what is knocking you.

- **The Law of Resistance**, whereby whatever you resist persists, because you are energizing it with your thoughts.

- **The Law of Projection**, where whatever you see in someone else is actually within you and you have projected it onto them.

- **The Law of Attachment**, which states that you can have what you want. However, if you desire an outcome conditionally, it prevents it from happening. The minute you let go, that person or situation is free to come to you or leave your life for your highest good.

The laws of creation

The second group of spiritual laws includes:

- **The Law of Attention**, which states that to the exact percentage you truly give your attention to something, it manifests. Positive thoughts have a more powerful charge than negative ones.

- **The Law of Flow**, which affects every area of your life, so if you declutter your home or workplace, stuck situations shift. Similarly, if you release clogged emotions or blocked thoughts, areas of your life clear.

- **The Law of Abundance**, which explains that everything you need is available to you and the benign universe wants you to have your heart's desire. When you align your beliefs and actions with what you desire, the doors of abundance open to you. When you are fifth-dimensional, your needs and wants are automatically granted.

- **The Law of Clarity**, which tells you that confusion keeps you stuck and uses up psychic energy, while a clear decision sets you free.

- **The Law of Intention**, which is very similar to the Law of Clarity, but with added force. A clear intention is like an arrow that aims for a target, and nothing can deflect it, so it is really important to know what you want.

- **The Law of Prosperity**, according to which you must align yourself to prosperity consciousness by thinking, talking and acting as if you already have plenty. You must also use your wealth responsibly. The universe wants us all to be prosperous.

- **The Law of Success**, which states that you achieve success when your vibration matches the vibration of your desired outcome. In material terms, your beliefs create your success, or lack of it.

In addition, there is *the Law of Manifestation*, which is often referred to as the Law of Attraction, but there is a difference. To activate the Law of Manifestation, you must focus wholeheartedly on what you want. You may draw it or talk about it as if you already have it, then visualize it going out into the universe. The next step is to imagine and feel as if it is in your life and act as if this is so. This is very powerful, so you must state you only wish your vision to manifest for the highest good of all. If you simply use the power for your own desires, you will draw your wish into your life, but you will also create karma. The power of the Law of Manifestation has been misused in recent years and this has held the whole planet back.

The laws of higher awareness

- **The Law of Balance and Polarity** reminds us of the importance of staying centred and also of looking at the aspects of our character that swing between polarities, for example being a bully and a victim, being generous and mean, being caring and negligent. When you recognize these aspects of yourself, you can bring yourself into balance.

- **The Law of Karma** is 'As you give, so you receive.' It plays out over generations and lifetimes and is coming to an end as we approach the fifth-dimensional new Golden Age.

- **The Law of Reincarnation** reminds you that your soul is on a long journey. If there is more for you to learn on Earth, you return again and again until you have mastered the spiritual laws.

- **The Law of Responsibility** makes clear that you are ultimately responsible for your every thought and action, including how you look after yourself and your small children. However, you are not responsible for anyone else, and if you take decisions for others, you bear any karma that results.

- **The Law of Discrimination** is particularly important at this time when so much misinformation is being spread. It tells you to follow your intuition and decide what is right for you.

- **The Law of Affirmation** makes clear that your mind acts like a computer. Every thought or word you keep repeating goes into it and programs it. So, it is essential to make positive statements and affirm who you are or who you want to be. You will become it.

- **The Law of Prayer** offers a reminder of the power of talking to God, for God always answers those who come from the heart and with pure intention. Sometimes, mercifully, He says, 'No.' But remember that when you ask, believing, it is already granted.

- **The Law of Meditation** reminds us of the power of listening to God; it states that when you quieten your mind, God has the opportunity to drop His ideas into it.

- **The Law of Challenge** is for your protection in the third-dimensional world of light and dark. If a being enters your space, under this law, if you ask, 'In the name of the Christ, are you of the purest and highest light?' three times, an honest answer must be given.

The laws of higher frequency

- **The Law of Frequency** states that people with higher vibrations positively influence those with lower vibrations.

- **The Law of Miracles** is very simple, for it reminds you that when you raise your vibration, anything can happen.

- **The Law of Healing** explains that when you bring through pure light, it transmutes lower energies and healing takes place.

- **The Law of Purification** reminds you that your aura is your protection and when it is totally pure, you are totally secure.

- **The Law of Perspective** declares that everything is divinely perfect, so if you don't like what you see, you must change your perspective.

- **The Law of Gratitude** explains that genuine appreciation opens people's hearts and it also opens the heart of God, who will bestow abundance on you.

- **The Law of Blessings** touches the person you bless with divine energy, and you also receive.

- **The Law of Decree** is very powerful, for your decree moves Heaven and Earth to do your bidding.

The transcendent laws for fifth-dimensional living

The three transcendent laws that Jesus brought forward for the ascension of humanity all those years ago are the same laws that we will live by in the new Golden Age. These are:

- **The Law of Faith**: Faith is the greatest power there is. If your intuition tells you that something is right, your unswerving faith in your vision makes it succeed.

- **The Law of Grace**: Grace is a divine dispensation of mercy and is conferred by qualities such as unconditional love, compassion, empathy and forgiveness.

- **The Law of One**: We are all one, so you cannot hurt another without hurting yourself.

There will also be sub-laws, such as the Law of Common Sense and the Law of Responsibility.

Monitoring society

What if someone does not act in a fifth-dimensional way? Will there be punishment or even prisons? No. These are not in accordance with the higher consciousness. There will be a recognition that we are all human, without judgement. The person will be surrounded in love, harmony and grace.

In the unlikely event of someone descending into third-dimensional activity, they will no longer wish to remain on Earth and will seek another planet where they can act out their drama.

The only guidance needed
will be the spiritual laws.

VISUALIZATION TO LIVE ACCORDING TO THE TRANSCENDENT LAWS

- Find a place where you can be quiet and undisturbed.

- Close your eyes and relax.

- Imagine what your life would be like if you had total faith in your vision.

- See a world where everyone has total faith in the goodness of humanity.

- Imagine what your life would be like if you acted with grace at all times.

- See a world where everyone acts with grace.

- See a world where everyone lives in the harmony of oneness.

- Take this feeling out into your daily life.

Chapter 19

Healing the Planet

Sadly, we have massively polluted the magnificent planet that is in our care, both since the Industrial Revolution and before, during the third experiment of Atlantis. However, with the rising consciousness and growing awareness of the damage we have done, we are trying to rectify this.

Nuclear pollution

The third experiment of Atlantis, long before the Golden Era arose, ended with a series of nuclear bombs being set off underground in a desperate effort to kill aggressive giant animals that had started to overrun the planet. The decision was reluctantly taken by a five-nation conference in 52,000bc, as they could not find a peaceful solution. It did kill the animals, but eventually humans too perished and returned to their home planets.

The nuclear residue from those bombs is still affecting Earth, and the Illumined Master Peter the Great has been working for aeons to clear the pollution. Now some scientists and elemental beings are co-operating with him. Also, spiritually awake humans are using the energy of prayer and visualization to accelerate the process, and this is more effective than anyone truly realizes.

Climate change

Climate change cannot be fully attributed to human activity, though. The climate on Earth has changed regularly over millions of years, during which we have had ice ages and arid times as well as pole shifts. The majority of the current changes are being caused by cosmic forces, as it is time for our world to change. Remember that in earlier ages, temperate forests used to grow in the area now covered by the frozen Antarctic. Everything changes.

Land that has been under the Arctic ice for aeons has been intentionally purified and prepared by the Intergalactic Council so that future civilizations can live there. The ice melting is resulting in rising sea levels and eventually many low-lying industrial cities that are not part of the new paradigm will be submerged. Some people in coastal areas will take action; for example, they will create floating towns that will become fifth-dimensional places to live, even golden cities.

All over the world there will be a move towards living in mountainous areas, for these have also been purified with snow and waterfalls.

New islands will rise up from the oceans. This land will have been cleansed by the waters and will be inhabited as soon as it is desalinated.

Change is happening very quickly as the new Golden Age approaches. However, there will not be a pole shift for at least 100 years.

Changes in the natural world

Many tree species are currently dying out because they can no longer cope with the changing climate. There are also contributory factors like pollution, stuck energy in the ley lines and – a factor that is little understood – lack of appreciation from humanity. Trees are sentient beings and are energetically responsive to humans. We have a two-way symbiotic relationship.

In the golden future, new tree species will appear that will be able to handle the different weather conditions. When the air is pure, the ley lines sparkle with fifth-dimensional light and we humans once more appreciate them, trees will stand tall and proud with radiant golden auras.

We will also really start to love and respect the animal kingdom. As the Golden Era progresses, new fifth-dimensional animals will incarnate and we will look after and honour them. They, too, will radiate golden auras.

Currently there are only four fifth-dimensional insect species. These are bees, butterflies, ants and ladybirds. There are only two fourth-dimensional insects: worms and scorpions. As the planet rises in frequency, more insects will raise their vibration. We will all learn to respect them and be grateful for the incredible work they do for us and the planet.

As the oceans and rivers once more become clean and pure, we will recognize and admire the marine life that maintains them. We will be particularly awed by the coral reefs, which will be protected and encouraged to spread. This living rock has an extraordinary two-way connection and communication flow with Hollow Earth. The reefs hold the ancient knowledge and wisdom of the planet and know everything about the oceans. All the fish that live within the coral reefs and look after it are fifth-dimensional.

World resources

Oil and minerals

The amount of fossil fuel that we have been karmically allowed to take from the planet was reached in 2012. The oil remaining in the ground is required for the lubrication of the tectonic plates. So, currently those who use it or profit from it are taking on karma. We have already seen some of the karmic consequences in the form of tsunamis and earthquakes. Indeed, big earthquakes have tripled in the 10 years since that date.

The way that we currently extract minerals from the ground is damaging the land. After 2032, new ways of doing so will be remembered that do not harm the planet. These harmless methods were used during the second Golden Age on Earth, the Age of Petranium, which was in Africa. During that time, Africa was lush and verdant. A memory of this too is held in our memory banks.

Food and water

By 2032, accessing enough food and water will be a challenge in some parts of the planet and we will be called on to look after one another. If we handle this in a fifth-dimensional way by opening our hearts, we can provide enough for all. Individuals and countries will be guided to move towards self-sufficiency.

During the great shift in consciousness between 2032 and 2050, we will learn to create pure and plentiful water from liquid hydrogen and quartz for the use of everyone.

Tree planting and reforestation

Already some towns are mindfully planting trees for the health and wellbeing of their citizens. Communities are starting to create orchards for the use of everyone, just as it will be in the golden future, but this is only just beginning to gain momentum.

Soon countries will co-operate to start reforesting the parts of the world that have been so badly depleted. When there is international peace and co-operation, this will accelerate.

Hedges and bushes will also be reinstated. When hedges were pulled up to make bigger fields for farmers and replaced by fences to create more room in gardens, the number of small birds declined.

Birds are only on Earth to teach, for they have nothing to learn. Hedgerow birds teach us about family life, and this rapidly declined as technology took over, as did the number of songbirds, who sing in the cosmic news for us.

As small birds diminished in number, predators swaggered in. A wave of crows, rooks and magpies poured into towns. This coincided with big businesses sweeping over the planet and swallowing up small businesses. The birds were mirroring to us what happens when we interfere with nature and reminding us of the importance of family life. As we start to nurture nature again, small birds will proliferate once more, and, reflecting this, families will communicate, play and love together once more.

Dustbowls will be refilled with vegetation, and arid countries like Australia will start serious reforestation programmes and reclaim the scrublands and deserts. This will change the climate of that continent, which will become more clement and temperate. This in turn will influence the people, who will also become gentler and more mellow.

And this trend will continue throughout the world.

Learning about nature

As the population declines, there will be more green space again. People will have more leisure and will explore the wonders of nature. So many of the sacred codes of the natural world have been forgotten, but those who retain the knowledge will come forward to teach both children and adults, and will rekindle the love for the land that is inherent in all of us.

In the golden future, from the earliest age children will learn about nature and the animal kingdom and be taught to respect them. Looking after pets will be encouraged, for this inculcates a sense of responsibility. It also teaches youngsters to understand and honour the needs of different species.

As reliance on allopathic medicine declines, many will once more want to learn about plants and herbs. Foraging will become a popular pastime.

We will no longer wish to impose our will on
nature and this will allow it to flourish.

VISUALIZATION FOR A HEALED PLANET

- Take a moment to close your eyes and relax.

- Imagine you are in a beautiful park.

- You look round and see that the trees, flowers, people, animals and land all have golden auras.

- You walk down a path and listen to the birdsong, smiling as you understand the birds' messages of encouragement and love.

- You connect heart to heart with the trees and receive positive qualities and energy.

- A stream tinkles beside you and the water is shimmering clear and silver.

- You feel totally safe and relaxed in the natural world.

- Know that nature is looking after you as you look after it.

Chapter 20

New Eco-Power Sources

By about 2034, when international peace has been established throughout the planet, we will be open and prepared to receive new free forms of eco-power. These will come from sources that we currently have no concept of. Scientists and technologists will be ready, albeit unconsciously, to work with angels and extraterrestrials to bring through new inventions. They will make extraordinary breakthroughs as they receive downloads of information from the higher realms.

Crystals

In the Golden Era of Atlantis, the Great Crystal received inputs of pure Source energy that powered all the crystals providing heat, light and power for the internet and other needs. For example, if you looked into the engine of a rocket, it would contain only a crystal.

In a very limited fashion we currently use crystals in memory chips in our computers and other technology. In the golden future, we will once more have the right consciousness to wake up different kinds of crystals. We will know how to work with their raw elemental power and their memory storage capacity.

Earth magnetism

The core of our planet is made up of liquid iron. As it cools and crystallizes, it stirs the molten metal, creating powerful electric currents. These flow through the outer core, generating a magnetic field that is so powerful, it stretches far out into space. This protects our planet in the same way that our aura protects us. It has incredible power and force, and if we were to utilize this energy without a fifth-dimensional consciousness of oneness, we would cause destruction. But as the Golden Age progresses, we will earn the right to harness this energy for free eco-power and will be taught how to do so.

Pyramid power

The pyramid is a cosmic shape that holds or creates energy. Scientists already know that the Great Pyramid of Giza can collect and concentrate electromagnetic energy in its chambers and at its base. When we are ready, the secrets of pyramid power will be revealed to us. Pyramids will not only provide free energy, but will be regeneration and rejuvenation chambers.

As already mentioned, the six cosmic pyramids are computers containing all the information and knowledge of Earth and this universe. They were programmed to start waking up in 2012 to activate the kundalini of our planet. As we rise in frequency, we will be able to understand and operate their incredible programs.

The oceans

In the golden future, we will look back in bemusement at the limited technology that enabled us to use hydro-electricity as a renewable power source. It will seem trivial when we eventually harness the awesome power of the oceans.

Lightning

Thunder and lightning are forces of nature that transmute lower energies. Thunder breaks up negativity above an area, including any that has been blown into that place. When this is transmuted, it is physically seen as sheet lightning. When it is transmuted into a positive force, it becomes fork lightning. This connects with the ley lines and is spread round the planet. In the golden future we will learn how to harness and use the free eco-power of this lightning.

The Sun

We currently harness solar power, but when we have the cosmic understanding and permission to reach through the Sun to the Great Central Sun, the source of all known light in this universe, we will access free power that we cannot even comprehend at this time. It will revolutionize the way we utilize the resources of the cosmos for travel and a million other things.

Wind

We have built wind turbines and think they are a solution for our future energy requirements. And in the future we will continue to use the force of the element air, but in a totally new way. As our consciousness expands, we will communicate with Dom, the elemental master of air, and co-operate with his elemental kingdom. When this happens, we will truly be able to manage and harness the wind for advanced electricity.

Plant energy

Every single thing that we need has been provided for us. Plants can literally be used in a million ways that we have never considered. In the golden future, we will learn how to turn them into any energy form that we need. We will do it in a way that honours the plant kingdom and meets our requirements in an ecological way without impacting on our food production.

Batteries

Soon after 2032, we will be able to store huge amounts of eco-power in small, light, compact batteries. This will obviate the need for cables or pipes and will be one of the many new inventions that will revolutionize our world.

Other forms of eco-power

The above list is but a sample of the possibilities that we can conceive. As the future is unimaginable to our current consciousness, there will be so much more than we can fathom now. There is so much to look forward to!

VISUALIZATION FOR A GOLDEN
FUTURE WITH FREE ECO-POWER

- Close your eyes and breathe comfortably.

- Imagine that all the power you need is freely available and is totally ecological.

- Your home can be as warm or as cool as you like.

- There is ample power for lighting, cooking and powering electric appliances.

- Eco-power charges your car.

- How does it feel to have all the power you need and how are you using it?

Chapter 21

Politics and Religion

In the era of Golden Atlantis, there were 12 regions, each overseen by a High Priest or Priestess who guided the people by teaching them the spiritual laws and inspiring them by example. They in turn received instructions from the Intergalactic Council.

Whether the citizens were in the priesthood or were part of the community, whatever they did, they were all considered equal. Men and women were equal, but with different roles, which they accepted as their soul choice and were happy to experience to the full.

Decisions were taken by consensus, with everyone acting for the highest good of all. In this way decisions were easily reached and everyone was happy.

During this era, there were no religions, only spirituality.

Ruled by masculine energy

For the past 10,000 years of masculine influence, however, many have tried to control others. They have fought for power and status without the balancing wisdom. As a result, most of the leaders who have thrust themselves to the fore have been those who sought to rise up the pyramids of power. This will change.

As we approach 2032, people of honour
and integrity will surface to empower
and inspire humanity into the new.

Female rule

Male energy without balancing feminine wisdom causes constant change. But female energy without the balancing masculine results in inertia. As a result, the women who have become leaders have ruled with male authority and qualities.

One of the few examples of true female governance has been the Aboriginal peoples, who grounded the energy of Lemuria to live on Earth as a separate experiment concurrent with Atlantis. They are a predominantly right-brained culture and embrace all the highest Divine Feminine qualities, ranging from sharing, peace and compassion to wisdom and continuity. They encourage continuity through stories and by taking collective responsibility for the land. Traditionally, decisions were made peacefully and collectively.

A true balance

By 2032, the masculine and feminine
energy on the planet will be balanced.

The Silver Ray

The move towards balance started in 2008, when the Silver Ray of the Divine Feminine returned to the planet for the first time in 10,000 years. This Ray is starting to light up the qualities of sharing, co-operation, supporting one another, working for the good of the whole rather than the individual, speaking from the heart, listening to understand, and inner wisdom.

We are rapidly moving towards a time of equality of the sexes. Men and women will be considered equal but different. Each will do what enriches them and gives them soul satisfaction.

The best qualities of the Divine Masculine and Feminine will balance internally and in relationships. People will develop power with wisdom, logic with intuition, protectiveness and trust, the ability to stand up for what they believe in and to co-operate for the good of the whole.

Both mind and heart will be respected.

Decision-making in the golden future

In the golden future oneness will prevail. In the fifth-dimensional consciousness, communities will automatically co-create for happiness and harmony. Decisions will easily emerge for the highest good.

Groups of people, whether in communities or representing countries, will gather together in peace. They will freely discuss issues and listen to one another. They will all see one another's energy fields, so everything will be open and honest, and they will all be attuned to their Higher Selves and will hold the intention of finding solutions or making decisions for the highest good of all, before all linking together heart to heart. In this way, decisions will be made quickly and easily, and everyone will be satisfied. This is the joy of oneness.

Religion and spirituality

We are all climbing a spiritual mountain. Some people join with others to follow a path guided by a particular leader who has laid down the route. These are religions. Each of these focuses on a different aspect of ascension. In their pure form, they are true guides, but all have been distorted.

Religions have played such an important part in humanity's journey during the last few thousand years that their essence will remain in the golden future, but the human construct around them will dissolve. Missionary religions have tried to influence or force others to join them, for example. This will no longer happen as we reclaim our individual authority.

Increasingly, individuals are already unconsciously seeing the beacon at the top of the mountain and are making their own way towards it.

There are several great illumined ones who are now helping religions to become more spiritual in preparation for the new Golden Age. Two of these are:

- **Mary Magdalene:** She was the spiritual partner of Jesus during their incarnation together and was a master in her own right. On the inner planes, she has become the Chohan of the Sixth Ray of Loving, Devoted Service in order to bring the influence of the Divine Feminine into religion. She is encouraging people to let go of old entrenched religious views and to make their own connection with Source. She is also bringing in new non-invasive healing methods for the new Golden Age.

- **Master Rakoczy:** An incarnation of St Germain, he is the Master of the 11th Ray of Clarity, Mysticism and Healing. His task is to bring peace and enlightenment into religions and into the minds of world leaders. He is also assisting us to manage pollution and to open up to the higher energies now available.

There is also a team of three great spiritual masters who are working to raise the spiritual frequency of humanity:

- **St Teresa of Avila**, who had an incarnation as a Spanish Carmelite nun, a mystic and spiritual writer living a contemplative and austere life. She is now an ascended master of the higher hierarchy, bringing oneness to religions.

- **St Catherine of Siena,** who incarnated as a lay member of the Dominican Order, who was also a mystic and author. Revered for her holiness and asceticism, she also had spiritual visions. She is now Lord of Karma for the 12th Ray and is helping to develop the spiritual light within humanity.

- **St Clare of Assisi,** who was once a follower of Francis of Assisi and founded the Order of Poor Clares. She is the twin flame of Lord Kuthumi, the World Teacher. As an ascended master of the higher hierarchy, she is bringing spiritual awareness to humanity.

VISUALIZATION FOR A GOLDEN FUTURE OF ONENESS

- Close your eyes and relax.

- Picture a spiritual mountain reaching up to the sky.

- There are many paths leading up the mountain and people are walking up these or making their own way up.

- You see that all the people, whatever their route, have qualities of love, harmlessness and oneness.

- They are all sharing and caring and freely helping one another.

- There is peace and acceptance everywhere.

- And at the top, they all step into glorious golden light.

Chapter 22

Gifts and Talents

In the Golden Era of Atlantis, everyone was telepathic and clairvoyant. In fact, videos could be sent from one person's third eye to another. If, for example, you wanted to know where your son was, you might send a telepathic question to him and receive a picture of him happily sailing with a group of friends. The Atlanteans could also heal and self-heal, and some could communicate with beings from other star systems. Their use of crystal technology was awesome, beyond our imagining.

They used 90 per cent of their expanded brain capacity. We use 10 per cent of our smaller brains.

In the next Golden Age, we will retrieve all the gifts, talents and powers we had in Golden Atlantis and move way beyond them into much higher frequencies.

2032 and soon after

By 2032, almost everyone will be fifth-dimensional and will have anchored their 12 chakras. Some will be at the upper levels of the fourth dimension, but will have their heart centres open, so the general high frequencies around them will help them ascend into the fifth dimension very quickly. Most significantly, our attitudes will be very different, for all our hearts will be open and we will be connecting to the spiritual realms.

Our gifts and powers are contained within the 12 strands of DNA that will start to connect and be activated when our 12 chakras are fully operational. This will enable us to open psychically and spiritually to some genetically encoded gifts while rapidly developing others.

Telepathy

Soon after 2032, most people will be telepathic, connecting mind to mind and receiving messages from each other. This is already happening, though it is often unconscious. People say, 'I was just thinking of you when you phoned,' or, 'You've just said what I was thinking.' Actually, they are telepathically tuning in to the other person.

There is already a huge interest in inter-species communication and soon we will all start to communicate mind to mind with animals. When people talk to their pets and say, 'My dog knows exactly what I want,' they already have a telepathic bond with their canine. Communicating telepathically with the animal kingdom will enrich our lives.

Telepathic communication with extraterrestrials and the angelic realms is also getting stronger. So many people contact me and tell me how they have received a strong impression that they must do something. They may say, 'It came into my mind that I must write a book,' and lots of ideas for it then flow in, or, 'The thought came to me that I must visit a certain person.' Usually something significant happens when they do, because their angel has communicated that they should go there.

All telepathic communications are pure, as there is no mental clutter or thoughtforms to distort them.

Clairaudience

This is different from telepathy, because you can actually hear a human voice.

This has only happened to me twice. The first time I was walking my dogs in my local woods and I saw someone I vaguely recognized, but I could not remember her name. Suddenly a clear voice said her name aloud! It was startling! I greeted her and she told me that she had had an urge to walk there. Her friend had suggested somewhere else, but she had strongly felt it had to be these woods. We became good friends and I feel that the spiritual realms were determined to draw this possibility to my attention.

The other occasion was really interesting and quite different. I had picked up my phone to make a call one day when I suddenly 'fell asleep'. I had actually moved into another dimension, though I was still in my sitting room.

In that dimension, my father, who had died over 20 years earlier, said as clearly as if he was in the room, 'Diana, how are you?' Interestingly, given our past history, his voice was full of love.

I replied, 'Fine, thanks,' then realized my father was on the other side. I quickly asked how he was and sensed a reply that he was all right. But the line was crackling and he was drawing away.

Then I returned to this dimension and there was no one in the room. I thought, *I miss you, Dad*. This surprised me, as I thought I had forgiven the past, but now I realized I had been angry with him for years! Suddenly I started to remember good things about him and my attitude to him shifted. The words 'I love you, Dad' came into my mind. It felt like a life-changing experience.

Clairaudience can be really important. I have talked to people who aren't usually clairaudient but have heard a voice warning them to avoid danger.

Clairsentience

This is where you tune in to the feelings, pain or emotions of another person. Many people do this unconsciously and take on that energy without knowing it. At the fifth-dimensional level, you simply tune in and empathize without taking the other person's energy into your own emotional or physical body.

Clairvoyance

In its purest form, this is seeing pictures about something that is out of conscious awareness or happening in the future. This ability will become more and more common as we start to accept our innate gifts, and soon after 2032 almost everyone will be able to see auras. This means that everything will be transparent and honest, for nothing can be hidden when your energy fields are visible.

As we start to see through the dimensions, we will become aware of the angelic realms too. Many people have been told from childhood that there are no such things as angels or fairies, that they are just figments of their imagination. In certain countries, this has been told to whole populations. Now everywhere people will rapidly awaken as they start to see these beings for themselves. When you have seen an angel, you cannot deny they exist! It will cause some confusion, even shock, as these societies experience a sudden profound shift in awareness.

As we start to see our guides and spiritual helpers, as well as ascended masters and beings from other star systems, it will be a huge revelation that massively raises the understanding and frequency on Earth.

Faith and trust will grow as we all start to see our own guardian angel and recognize just how much help is available to us. And many people will be aware of the archangels guiding and assisting us. We will see the dragons of air, earth, fire and water, plus dragons from other realms, all looking out for us. Many will see unicorns, great pure beings of light who often appear as white horses with a horn of light, and realize just how much they do to hold our frequencies high. When we garden or walk out in nature, we will be aware of the nature spirits, too, and all the elemental kingdoms.

Intuition

Intuition is a function of the third eye, knowing without actually seeing a picture. It can come as a flash or an inner knowing and will become more honed as we recognize how important it is to trust ourselves.

Claircogniscence

This is suddenly receiving a download of spiritual information, a concept or revelation. These inspirations will be acknowledged and respected as the frequency rises.

Healing and self-healing

As the fifth-dimensional chakras are established in everyone, we will all be able to access healing energy from the spiritual realms. Anyone who chooses to do so will be able to give healing too. However, as happens now, many will choose to focus on and develop other gifts.

More individuals will bring higher frequencies through for their own self-healing.

Artistic and creative gifts

As with all other gifts, as our frequency rises, our artistic and creative channels will expand and inspiration will flow through. This will be a liberation for many.

Channelling

People will be more and more in touch with the higher realms of guides, angels and stellar beings. Inspiration, inventions and information will commonly be brought through.

By 2050

Everyone will be telepathic. Phones will be totally redundant, as communication between humans and other species will be clear and unambiguous. Everyone will be clairvoyant, so there will be total transparency, honesty and integrity, with the attendant feelings of trust and safety.

Artistic and creative endeavours will be extraordinary.

While there will be healing temples, most people will be able to self-heal, so the masses will be vibrantly healthy.

VISUALIZATION TO RECEIVE YOUR GIFTS

- Take a moment to relax, close your eyes and breathe comfortably.

- Picture yourself with your family or friends, communicating telepathically, clearly and honestly.

- What do you send and receive? How does this feel?

- You understand how those around you feel, so you have empathy with them.

- Be aware that you can see into the spiritual realms in a way that is beautiful and comfortable for you.

- Open up to receive guidance from the angelic realms.

- Your body is vibrantly healthy.

- You know that if there is ever an imbalance or you injure yourself, you can self-heal.

- Open your eyes and bring this into your physical life.

Chapter 23

Powers and the Perfected Human

At the height of the Golden Era of Atlantis, people could levitate, teleport and manifest objects. These powers will become commonplace once more in the golden future.

Powers

Levitation

Levitation is currently considered the ability to float in the air in your physical body. By 2040, more and more people will be able to control their energy fields so that they can rise up and then transport themselves. This power will be harnessed for short distances, for example if you want to cross a river without a bridge or glide to your neighbour's house. Though the more accessible this becomes, the more people will prefer to exercise their bodies by walking.

Teleportation

In the golden future, people will be able to teleport, in other words dematerialize their physical body through time and space and rematerialize somewhere else. During this process, the cellular structure of the body breaks down into an atomic energy stream. You become pure light and can travel along the ley lines. Then you can rematerialize at your intended destination. This process overcomes gravity.

Currently some people do this unconsciously. Usually someone tells you that you have appeared and spoken to them, but you have no recollection of it. In the golden future, those who teleport will be consciously aware of what they are doing.

Apportation

Apports are things you move from one place to another without physically fetching and carrying them. This will become a commonplace power and very useful. For example, if you are gardening, you can apport a trowel into your hand from a distance without getting up. If you are hungry, you can draw fruit from a branch right into your hands.

Manifestation

Many people will be able to manifest objects, in other words draw things from the unmanifest world into the physical one. In each community, groups of people who specialize in this power will meet to manifest things that are needed for the collective. These can be anything from chairs to vehicles. The people will connect heart to heart with the intention of creating for the highest benefit of everyone, then use the power of their navel chakra to draw the vision they hold up into their Soul Star chakra, where it will be radiated out at a very high frequency in order to bring about a physical reality. This technique will become part of the natural abundance we enjoy.

Mind control

Everyone, even young children, will be taught mind control and will practise it in order to develop their powers. Advanced control, including over their energy fields, will allow people to manage their body in ways that we cannot yet conceive.

At the same time, the ability to work with and manipulate the energies of the universe will confer extraordinary powers. Everyone will have the integrity and high consciousness that allow this to be.

El Morya, the perfected human

The Manu, or perfected human, has stepped forward into this role. The great master El Morya is the Manu for the sixth root race of humanity. This means that his cells, his chakras and energy fields hold the keys and codes of the next spurt of human evolution. With 12 strands of DNA connected and active, he carries incredible gifts and powers, and connects with cosmic wisdom. He demonstrates all that we can be.

El Morya is one of the mighty illumined ones and originates from Mercury, the planet of higher communication and truth. He understands the trials of human incarnation and has ascended through many initiations. This is why he has been chosen to be the Manu for the next step in our advancement.

He has always been interested in the flow of the cosmos and, as a High Priest in Atlantis, he studied the stars and planets. He was an advanced astronomer and astrologer. He had a deep understanding of the way in which we and our planet are influenced by the movements of the universe. He worked with the Universal Angel Butyalil, who is in overall charge of the cosmic currents and ensures that all is in divine order.

When Atlantis fell, El Morya took his tribe to the area now known as Iraq. Here he founded the Mesopotamian civilization, settling round the Euphrates river. He enabled the Mesopotamians to develop their script, which they learned to record on clay tablets. He also studied and discovered the cosmic qualities of water and realized that it could transmute and dissolve karma as well as carry Christ Light. With this knowledge, he brought forward the concept of baptism.

Another very significant lifetime was as Melchior, one of the Three Wise Men. The other two were Lord Kuthumi and Djwhal Khul. All were highly evolved and trained Magi with significant powers. As an astrologer, Melchior was able to forecast the birth of Jesus. The Three Wise Men then travelled to his birthplace, arriving before Mary and Joseph, so that they could support Jesus as he incarnated for his mission to bring the Christ Light to Earth.

In another noteworthy lifetime, El Morya was Abraham, who founded the Jewish religion. This aspect of his soul is a great dragon master who trains others to be dragon masters. As Abraham, he is now Lord of Karma of the 10th Ray.

He was also Akbar the Great, a wise ruler known for his religious tolerance, who rewarded talent and loyalty regardless of ethnicity. In that lifetime he helped to unify India.

He was King Arthur and King Solomon, both respected for their wisdom.

Co-operating with Lord Kuthumi, he impressed Madame Blavatsky to found the Theosophical Society.

Currently he is Master of the First Ray of Divine Will and Creation, the bright red ray of power and purpose. One of the important lessons that he brings to us through this ray is to follow our divine will rather than our desires.

He is also a member of the Intergalactic Council, where his role is to strengthen people's will so that humanity can actively co-create the new age. He is very busy assisting us to break down old third-dimensional structures and at the same time offers us opportunities for ascension by giving us glimpses of higher possibilities for the golden future.

He is working with Archangels Michael and Faith to balance the masculine and feminine energy in individuals to prepare us for the new golden future. He is also bringing the Divine Masculine and Feminine energy on Earth into equilibrium.

In addition, he is a member of the White Brotherhood. (White stands for purity and truth.) There are several branches of the White Brotherhood, including the Cathars, Essenes, Rosicrucians and others. El Morya understands the mystery teachings of the Great White Brotherhood, who hold the secrets of perfect peace and eternal life.

He has two etheric retreats on the inner planes above Earth, one over Calcutta and the other over Kashmir. You can take an inner journey to connect with him more easily in these places.

Imagine El Morya visiting your community. What would you like to discuss with him?

The gifts and powers we will have by 2050

By 2050, everyone will have reached the higher levels of the fifth dimension and have their 12 chakras fully established. Everyone will be able to levitate, float above the ground for short distances and apport objects to themselves. All will use focused thought to bring objects from the unmanifest world into the physical one. This will only ever be done for the highest good of all.

Within communities, groups will gather with pure intention to draw the communal needs into physicality. We will, for example, manifest building materials using sound and mind control. Together, we will be able to create wonderful and beneficial things for all.

We will also use sound and crystal technology to control the weather for the benefit of everyone. We will fully understand the powers of crystals and will program them once more to help humanity.

By 2050, every single thing will be biodegradable and we will have the ability to dematerialize rubbish and waste. Because we will wrap all items in ecological re-usable materials that we have not invented yet, there will be very little waste in any case. We will have new ways of producing fresh foods throughout the year and currently unimagined cooling methods, so there will be no need for cumbersome refrigerators or freezers.

We will use our power to purify the earth and the oceans. Water for drinking and in rivers and oceans will be purified with advanced frequency waves sent through crystals and we will also be able to create pure water from its elements.

Our current internet will be a joke! The free advanced quantum internet will be for the benefit of everyone. It will allow enormous amounts of information to be transmitted instantly and reliably on high-frequency wavelengths that we have not yet accessed, and these will have bonuses for humanity. Only spiritual, joyous, truthful and inspirational material will be transmitted, for this will reflect the consciousness of the people.

By 2050, most people will have new, lighter bodies, and all children will have the larger brain capacity of the perfected human, with their 12 strands of DNA connected. By that time, huge changes will have taken place on Earth, beyond our current imagination. Every single thing will be on a much higher frequency.

By 2050, the world
will be unrecognizable.

VISUALIZATION TO EXPERIENCE YOUR GIFTS IN THE GOLDEN FUTURE

- Sit quietly and close your eyes.

- Imagine you are already living in the golden future.

- Your 12 chakras are radiating beautifully and your 12 strands of DNA are connected.

- Sense yourself being able to levitate. Does this feel familiar?

- Now sense yourself teleporting from one location to another. How does this feel? How do you use it?

- Imagine a group around you. Together, you are manifesting something for your golden community. See this happening.

- Know that if a gift or power feels familiar, it is already encoded within you.

- Open your eyes and smile.

- You are living in a world where you can use the power of your mind to change matter or draw material things to you. What do you do with this ability?

Part III

Preparing for the Fifth Dimension

Chapter 24

Your Spiritual Foundation for Higher Ascension

We humans have the power to make the transition to this wondrous future slow and painful for ourselves or to bring it about quickly and easily. It is entirely up to every single one of us.

In this part I am sharing the lessons you need to understand, experience or master in each chamber of each chakra in order to prepare not only for the golden future, but for higher ascension into the upper levels of the fifth dimension. I suggest you read these carefully, for when you explore them, you may choose to pursue different activities in your life.

Just talking or thinking of the lessons of these spiritual centres with focus and higher intent often allows the chambers to open and awaken. The vibration of your thoughts or words may be enough to shift any energy that needs to be dissolved. Also, as you pay attention to each chamber, the archangel in charge of that chakra may switch on the light in that particular room.

As you read the lessons, ask for anything you need to experience or understand to be presented to you. The lesson or awareness will come to you in a perfect way. If you ask with genuine intent, your soul and your Monad will ensure it comes into your life. You may sense that you have opened that door in another incarnation.

When you are finally ready to fully awaken your blazing fifth-dimensional chakras, Archangel Metatron will help you with the process. One of his incredible ascension tools is the Metatron Cube, and he can use it as a key to burst open locked doors then unwind and clear energy stuck behind them. The Metatron Cube can then be activated to fill a chakra with light of a higher frequency than it has ever experienced before. (There is a picture of the Metatron Cube on page 251.)

When you have reached a sufficient level of light, even if it is only for a moment, the sixth-dimensional chakra column can slip down into your body, and sometimes even the seventh-dimensional one.

This is because we are now moving to a frequency that is higher than ever before and those on the higher ascension path are being prepared to light the way for the world.

The Earth Star chakra

A strong spiritual foundation is as
important as the solid underpinning of
a skyscraper! You need it to ascend.

Your fifth-dimensional spiritual foundation is your Earth Star chakra. It is about 30 cms (12 inches) below your feet and is overseen by Archangel Sandalphon. When it first anchors, it is black and white, then as it establishes, it becomes grey, then liquid silver, the colour of the ultimate Divine Feminine. Silver also reflects Archangel Sandalphon's ninth-dimensional light.

Your Earth Star chakra grounds you fully into Gaia
and contains your fifth-dimensional blueprint. When

you are born, your life mission is programmed into it,
so it holds your life purpose and your divine potential.

Lady Gaia, the great angel in charge of Earth, and our planet itself hold Divine Feminine energies, so the spiritual foundation that plugs you deep into Earth for your lifetime is feminine. Here lies your kundalini, your life-force.

For 10,000 years, the kundalini of the planet was held in the Gobi Desert by Sanat Kumara as a masculine energy. In 2008, in preparation for the new Golden Age, the Mayan elders moved it to Archangel Sandalphon's retreat at Lake Atitlan in South America. They transformed it by divine alchemy into a feminine energy. This place was chosen to house the kundalini because South America is connected to the planet Venus, where the Divine Feminine and pure love essence of this universe is held. This allows our planetary kundalini to be imbued with love from the Cosmic Heart.

The Divine Feminine is the route to peace on Earth and also in your personal life.

The kundalini of the planet is part of the Divine
Feminine blueprint held in your spiritual foundation.

Carefully monitored by Archangel Sandalphon, this chakra helps your vibration to rise in tune with the rising frequency of the planet.

The establishment of this spiritual foundation
in as many people as possible is vital so that
peace can spread and the masses can ascend into
the fifth dimension for the new Golden Age.

Your spiritual foundation is also your doorway to Hollow Earth, the seventh-dimensional paradise where Lady Gaia dwells. It is where your invitation from Lady Gaia for this incarnation is held. It is the link between your spiritual self and your earthly self, for it is only when your spiritual self is grounded that your Stellar Gateway chakra can open.

When your Earth Star chakra is established, it guides you to the location where you are meant to be.

Planetary and cosmic Earth Star chakras

The Earth Star chakra of our planet is in London. It is almost fully open, but needs a burst of Divine Feminine light to fully raise its frequency. It is connected to Hollow Earth, where there is a Golden Crystal Pyramid that is a seventh-dimensional light source. Here the mighty Master Serapis Bey holds the connections to every single Earth Star chakra. It is as if he is holding the strings of millions of silver balloons and they are being plugged into the charger, the Golden Crystal Pyramid. When every single Earth Star chakra is established and billions of them glow silver, our planet will truly radiate.

The cosmic Earth Star is Neptune and the part that has already ascended is called Toutillay. Here the cosmic blueprint for this universe is held, as well as many keys to the full ascension of this universe into the fifth dimension. When your spiritual foundation is fully activated, you can connect to Toutillay to access knowledge and wisdom from Lemuria and Atlantis.

Establishing your spiritual foundation

Your Earth Star chakra contains 33 lessons or chambers. Some of these you may already have mastered in other incarnations. You may be surprised how simple and natural many of them are. Take the journey now, and as you carefully read the lesson of each chamber, Archangel Sandalphon will be with you, helping you to heal, light up, activate or integrate the lesson.

- **Chamber 1:** To awaken the first chamber, actively notice and honour what a beautiful and extraordinary planet we live on.

- **Chamber 2**: Actively look for the beauty that is everywhere. Appreciate it and enjoy it.

- **Chamber 3**: When you walk, be consciously aware that you are giving your energy to the planet and at the same time you are receiving energy from it. Think about the film *Avatar*, where the footsteps of the Na'vis light up when they connect lovingly with their planet, Pandora. We have a similar two-way connection with Earth.

- **Chamber 4**: Bring light down through your 12 chakras and consciously pour it into Earth. Even better, make your chakras into a column of light that extends into Earth and opens this chamber.

- **Chamber 5**: Earth loves you. She wants to give to you, and this chamber opens when you allow yourself to receive her love.

- **Chamber 6**: Everything that grows in the earth has a purpose and is a gift. Respect all greenery, whether or not you understand its purpose. If you pull out a weed, do it graciously. Honour the produce of the earth and bless your food, so that this chamber opens.

- **Chamber 7**: This lesson is learned when you dig in the soil and feel its energy as well as its texture. If you live in an apartment and have no access to the soil, you can plant herbs or plants in pots to get in touch with the earth. Or you may have done this in another life.

- **Chamber 8**: Trees are wise sentient beings, holding much knowledge as well as serving us in many practical ways. Touch them when you can. Notice them and mentally honour them.

- **Chamber 9**: Plant trees. If you cannot physically do so, gather acorns or chestnuts, or beech or hazelnuts, or any other tree fruits, and spread them where you can.

- **Chamber 10**: Enjoy the experience of walking barefoot on the grass. This is a wonderful way to connect with Earth and it awakens the light in this chamber.

- **Chamber 11**: Flowers carry the essence of divine love, and wherever they are, they radiate light and beauty to raise the frequency in the vicinity. The lesson of this chamber is to acknowledge and honour them for who they truly are. At the same time, mentally thank the fairies who look after them.

- **Chamber 12**: All water carries the Christ Light and spreads it everywhere. The seas and oceans are vast reservoirs of love and wisdom that help to hold the frequency of the planet high. When you appreciate and honour water, this chamber will radiate pure light.

- **Chamber 13**: Within the air is *prana*, the life-giving breath of Source. It is your connection to God. In recognizing this, you unlock the door to this chamber.

- **Chamber 14**: Fire is a vibrant and powerful element. It can transmute lower energies right down to a cellular level. This chamber opens when you truly honour its transmuting qualities.

- **Chamber 15**: Earth is our mother. She provides a veritable cornucopia of delight to nurture us. To awaken this chamber, tune in to and be grateful for just how much abundance she offers you.

- **Chamber 16**: Like us, animals come from the stars with a soul mission and life purpose. They have incarnated to experience, learn and teach with the right brain. Understand and respect these amazing beings and see them for who they truly are.

- **Chamber 17**: Reptiles incarnate from all over the universes and step down through the spiritual plane of Neptune, carrying their original divine blueprints. Many spread the seventh-dimensional energy of Hollow Earth wherever they go. When you look at them with higher perception and honour them, this chamber bursts open.

- **Chamber 18**: Birds are messengers for angels and are only here to teach, for they have nothing to learn. This chamber is fully awake when you honour them and are aware of their messages.

- **Chamber 19**: Marvel at the greenery of nature and the incredible process of photosynthesis that allows leaves to harness sunlight for nourishment and release oxygen.

- **Chamber 20**: Rocks and stones are wise keepers of ancient history and they hold the secrets of the growth of our planet. When you really wonder at them, this chamber opens up.

- **Chamber 21**: Crystals are concentrated forms of light that amplify energy, including healing. They gather information, store it and release it. The doors of this room open wide when you recognize who they truly are and send healing to the place where they have been dug out.

- **Chamber 22**: We live in an amazing and diverse universe. The millions of stars and planets are all interconnected, all radiating and sharing light. When you accept that each one is impacting on Earth and relevant to your life, this part of the Earth Star chakra magically opens.

- **Chamber 23**: Dolphins are the wise ones of the oceans. They are the High Priests and Priestesses of the water worlds, holding the knowledge and wisdom of the Golden Era of Atlantis. The information they hold is beyond anything that we can currently understand. Know this and accept the lessons of joy, peace, higher healing and oneness that dolphins radiate, in order to tune in to the lesson of this chamber.

- **Chamber 24:** All marine life is serving the oceans in some way. Some spread Christ Light, others purify the waters and a few bring in the knowledge and wisdom of the stars. When you know that each one is fulfilling an amazing purpose, you can tune in to the secrets of this chamber.

- **Chamber 25:** Every human is on Earth by invitation from Lady Gaia. Some are incredibly evolved beings disguised in bodies of flesh. Others are newcomers adjusting to an alien world. Every single one is doing their best in often challenging circumstances, so whatever they are doing or however they appear, accept and honour them all.

- **Chamber 26:** This section of the Earth Star chakra lights up when you accept oneness – that everything and everyone is part of God. This includes people and situations that you do not like, for all are learning about love.

- **Chamber 27:** The Sun represents the Divine Masculine power in this universe. Next time you see it, consciously thank it and honour it.

- **Chamber 28:** The Moon represents the Divine Feminine qualities of this universe. Next time you see it, consciously thank it and honour it.

- **Chamber 29:** The pyramids were built by great masters, overseen by archangels. They hold great wisdom and knowledge, especially the six cosmic pyramids – those in Egypt, Mexico,

Tibet, Mesopotamia, Peru and Greece. These six are cosmic computers, generators and substations for universal energy. Some have been destroyed physically, but are active in the ether. All are connected to different star systems and are portals for their light. When you understand this, you light up this chamber in your Earth Star chakra.

- **Chamber 30**: Mountains are ancient sentient beings. Like all living things, they emit a sound. Some peaks sing high clear angelic notes so pure that they radiate harmony over a wide area. At the same time, they purify and raise the frequency. Crystals and gemstones within mountains sing their own songs, and these add to the harmonic range. Honour these rugged crags, for this is the lesson of this chamber.

- **Chamber 31**: Forests are known as the lungs of the planet. They are also record-keepers and hold and anchor ancient wisdom. They stabilize countries energetically. In addition, they are portals that bring in the light from other stars and planets and store it until we are ready to accept it. Recognize this and you have learned the lesson of this chamber.

- **Chamber 32**: We vibrate on a particular frequency and are surrounded and interspersed by spiritual beings on dozens of other frequencies. The angelic realms and illumined ones vibrate at a faster rate than we do, so they may be beyond our range of sight and hearing. Nevertheless, they are amongst us and trying to assist us. This part of your Earth Star chakra awakens when you recognize this and honour the spiritual world and the angelic energy within you.

- **Chamber 33**: There are many dimensions beyond the physical and this chakra fully opens when you accept this.

VISUALIZATION TO BUILD A DEEP SPIRITUAL FOUNDATION

- Close your eyes, take a deep breath and relax.

- Focus on your silver Earth Star chakra below your feet.

- See roots moving down from it to connect deeply to the heart of Lady Gaia.

- Sense how deeply connected to Earth you are.

- Draw up the beautiful gentle Divine Feminine energy into your Earth Star chakra.

- Feel this compassionate, caring, loving energy becoming the foundation for nurturing your spiritual journey.

- See or sense a fountain of a beautiful spiritual light rising from your Earth Star and moving right up through your chakra system to your Stellar Gateway.

- Look up at the stars sparkling in the dark sky and feel their wisdom awaiting you.

- Sense or listen to the Music of the Spheres and let their influence seep into you.

- Focus again on your Earth Star and notice how it has changed.

Chapter 25

Building a Solid
Support System

A solid support system is not just good for your health and welfare; feeling safe, secure and balanced Is important for your spiritual life. It is part of the preparation for the golden future when people everywhere will automatically co-operate to help one another.

Practical scaffolding

Several things form the practical scaffolding of your days. Your family, friends and neighbours are your most vital assistants in times of challenge. The new Golden Age focuses on sharing, caring and rich relationships. The more you can participate in and encourage the creation of a local caring community, the safer you feel and the more your base chakra can relax. Forming friendship groups, getting to know your neighbours and contributing to community togetherness are not just social assets, but also enhance your spiritual growth.

Your home life and where you live also have a huge influence on you. The job you do and your work environment affect your sense of satisfaction too. So do your hobbies.

Feeling relaxed and good about these areas of your life enables your base chakra to spin freely.

*Your base chakra is the ground floor of your
ascension skyscraper, while your Earth
Star forms your deep foundation.*

The base chakra

Safe and rooted

Your base chakra is located at the base of your spine. For 10,000 years, the base chakras of humanity have been focusing on keeping people safe by sending out antennae to check that they will survive. They sought reassurance that the family was safe or looked for employment or shelter. If they spun too fast in their efforts to search out danger, people became anxious, or if they moved too slowly, people became depressed. If they tensed up, the base of the spine tightened and people experienced lower back pain.

Now more and more people are establishing their fifth-dimensional base centre, which is a beautiful shining platinum light.

Taking care of earthly matters helps to consolidate your base chakra, while spiritual practices enable it to connect smoothly to your Earth Star. Your chakras are interconnecting cogs or wheels, so the more effortlessly they work together, the more light can flow through all your systems.

If something does not feel right in your life, this centre is stuck. Consider what changes you can make, for your root reflects the practical basis of your incarnation. It is in the charge of Archangel Gabriel, and one of his tasks is to help you make clear decisions. If you take one that elevates your life, he will assist you in its fulfilment.

*Your fifth-dimensional base chakra seeks balance in
your life and high-frequency sustenance for you.*

Good food, pure drinking water and appropriate exercise help to solidify and consolidate your energy on every level – physical, mental, emotional and spiritual. They underpin all that you do on Earth, and they particularly affect your base. Touching the earth, for example by walking, especially in bare feet, helps to anchor and purify this centre. However, if you walk on tarmac or concrete, you cannot draw in the life-force of Gaia.

Hugging a tree or sitting under it with your back against the trunk immediately soothes and raises the frequency of this chakra. This enables it to relax and spin in rhythm with your other chakras.

With the platinum root in place, your back relaxes and energy flows into your feet chakras, which open up to receive support and wisdom from your Earth Star. Your root also accepts a flow of light from your higher chakras.

Planetary and cosmic base chakras

The base chakra of our planet is in Mongolia, China.

The cosmic base chakra is Saturn, and the aspect of Saturn that has already ascended is called Quichy. The capital of our solar system is on Saturn and it is run by the Council of Nine, which is an advanced group consciousness. There are actually 12 masters of Saturn, but three are beyond the reach of our frequency. The Council of Nine helps to administer the spiritual laws of our universe.

The following mighty illumined ones are affecting us through our base chakras:

- **Master Marko**, who represents the highest galactic confederation in our solar system, is helping to bring forward the positive energies of Saturn through the base chakras of humanity. These are qualities such as power, discipline, hard work and commitment. Also the ability to deal with change, as well as the responsibilities of wealth and fame.

- **Lord Hilarion** is the negotiator for Earth on the Council of Saturn and he helps us remain true to our spiritual journey.

- **Master Merlin** also represents the Council of Saturn. His task is to help humanity foster the discipline needed for magic and alchemy. This will be very much needed as we approach the golden future, when mind control will be developed not just for magic and alchemy, but also healing and manifestation.

The petals or chambers of the base chakra

This chakra has two chambers only and each is dedicated to living in a grounded and balanced way on the planet. To prepare you for ascension, they aim to bring into equilibrium your masculine and feminine energy.

As already noted, the planetary consciousness for the last century has made it impossible for anyone to have had totally wise, balanced, loving parents. However, you can create your own internal ones and this will enable you to bring your root chakra fully into the fifth dimension.

Just imagine you have a mother who feels safe and independent. She is confident and feels good about herself. She is always loving, nurturing, caring, supportive, kind and compassionate.

And your father feels safe and independent. He too is confident and has good self-worth. He is always strong, protective, supportive, reliable and proud of you.

You can add any other qualities that are important to you, for example consistency, logic, calmness or trustworthiness. With these balanced parents in your head, your self-talk brings you into harmony and equilibrium. You feel confident, safe and trusting. And your base chakra glows platinum.

The journey to mastery

Your base chakra is often described as the Seat of the Soul. Just as your Earth Star chakra works in alignment with your Stellar Gateway, so your base chakra is connected to your Soul Star. When your base is fully fifth-dimensional, it expands until it encapsulates your Soul

Star. Then the energy of your soul illuminates your base and anchors into it. You can achieve enlightenment and your ascension journey is accelerated.

Your platinum base chakra

When your base chakra starts to radiate platinum light, you have total trust in the universe to keep you safe and secure and provide for all your needs. This faith and sense of security enables you to flow with joy and harmony, which in turn attracts good circumstances to you. You take responsibility for your life and apply self-discipline. These are the qualities for mastery and enable you to ascend. You are also able to develop good spiritual practices.

As this centre becomes more and more radiant, light flows through all your chakras and this helps to build your Antakarana bridge to Source. You connect with the masters of Saturn and receive guidance from those Illumined Beings. You also become closer to Archangel Gabriel and he helps you connect with the sacred wisdom of the dolphins.

Dolphins are the wise ones of the planet and keepers of cosmic knowledge. They are the High Priests and Priestesses of the oceans and help to hold the frequency of the waters high. The Intergalactic Council placed the wisdom and knowledge of the Golden era of Atlantis into them, and they hold it like a computer. They download it to you when you are ready to receive it.

Archangel Gabriel's message

Archangel Gabriel and his twin flame, Archangel Hope, are constantly beaming light into your base chakra to strengthen and sustain you. Allow yourself to receive this.

Archangel Gabriel has a message for you:

'Be on the planet but not of it.'

Because your spiritual grounding is also intensely practical, Archangel Gabriel is asking you to be aware of what is happening around you on your personal journey and also in the world. However, do not give energy to anything that does not support your fifth-dimensional essence. Enjoy the experiences that life offers you. Make the most of this opportunity. Yet always remain connected to your spiritual knowing.

VISUALIZATION TO BALANCE
YOUR BASE CHAKRA

- Picture yourself in the pure, high mountains of Mongolia, China, the base chakra of the planet.

- Your wise mother, like a High Priestess, stands in front of you and tells you all the supportive things you need to hear.

- Then your wise father, like a High Priest, tells you all the supportive things you need to hear from him.

- See yourself standing tall, strong, joyful and confident.

- The portal to Saturn and Quichy opens and the Council of Nine address you. What message do they have for you?

- When you return, take the time to relax and swim in beautiful, clear blue waters with dolphins.

- Finally see or sense your base chakra radiating shining platinum light.

Chapter 26

Attracting Your Soul Family and Embracing Higher Sexuality

We are rapidly progressing towards the golden future when, for the first time since the fall of Atlantis, we can all experience true love. We have the opportunity now to create good family relationships and at last we can meet and be nurtured by our soul family. We are moving towards joyful, respectful sexuality or even the transcendent expression of sexual love.

All this happens when we raise the
frequency of our sacral chakra and balance
the masculine and feminine energy.

The sacral chakra

Your sacral chakra contains 16 lessons. These are all to do with relationships, especially with your family, and sexuality. When you attract a relationship at a third-dimensional level, it is usually only a physical connection. At the fifth dimension, this chakra seeks transcendent love.

During this incarnation and probably many others, most of us have sent and received lower thoughts, and these have created cords that have clogged this centre. We are ready for these to be finally transmuted. It is also time to clear out anger, as well as individual and collective sexual guilt. Here is a forgiveness affirmation to help you:

I forgive myself for any lower thoughts, words or actions in this life or any other. I forgive others for their lower thoughts towards me that form cords to me.

Currently a massive clear-out of this centre is taking place, as revelations of all kinds are being drawn to our attention. When lightworkers refrain from judging and instead send love and light into the collective cloud of relationship imbalance and sexual guilt, this will raise the frequency of the sacral. As we do this together, we are accelerating a shift in the planetary collective consciousness to one of mutual health and empowerment between men and women. This will spread to everyone and transform the world.

When you express pure love, your sacral chakra glows with glorious fifth-dimensional delicate golden pink light, so that you attract empowering, loving, respectful relationships.

As the sacral chakras of humanity become fifth-dimensional, more and more people will attract their soul families to them. By 2032, babies will be born into their soul families rather than those that trigger their karmic lessons. Relationships will be based on unconditional love, joy and mutual respect. Everyone will be free and independent.

The sacral and navel chakras

During the Golden Era of Atlantis, the sacral was separate from the navel chakra, which is above it.

After the fall, as the 12 fifth-dimensional chakras were replaced by seven lower-frequency ones, the navel was withdrawn. The third-dimensional sacral that remained carried some of its qualities. But now the navel is being returned in its full glory.

While these two chakras are currently separate, each with 16 lessons, they are encapsulated in a vast chamber, which is the 33rd lesson.

Planetary and cosmic sacral chakras

The sacral of Earth is Honolulu. The cosmic sacral is Sirius, and the part that has ascended is Lakumay. There has been a recent upgrade, and now the Golden Globe containing ninth-dimensional Christ Light is held in Sirius, while 11th-dimensional Christ Light is available in Lakumay, so that transcendent love pours into Honolulu and spreads round the world. It is healing the sacral chakras of humanity, so that by 2032 we will be expressing pure love through sexuality.

Archangel Gabriel

The mighty, pure white Archangel Gabriel is in charge of the development of your sacral chakra. He brings love, joy, clarity, hope and purity to this chakra and helps to raise the frequency there. He also brings it into perfect yin–yang, masculine–feminine balance.

Ask him to help you bring it into equilibrium and sense him placing a yin–yang symbol there.

The lessons of the sacral chakra

Here are the lessons we have to learn in order to bring relationships, sexuality and true love to a higher octave. Remember that you may have learned some of these during other incarnations.

As more people anchor their 12 fifth-dimensional chakras, it becomes evident when this one is out of balance. The tests of the first five chambers are for those who are focused on self. As you read through them, you may find thoughts or images surfacing. Don't judge them, just let them emerge, for this is part of the healing process.

You may find a hurt inner child in some or all of these rooms. A hurt child can become manipulative, needy, greedy or frightened. They may feel unfulfilled or scared of emotional attachment. And a hurt child can be cruel. Paedophiles and stalkers are stuck here. Unlovable as a hurt child seems, they need love, attention and understanding, so whatever arises for you, take a moment to listen to and hug your inner child.

- **Chamber 1**: The first chamber is about using sexuality for control. If you have ever said 'No' to love-making because you were angry or hurt, or as a way to get money or a favour from your partner, you may find a hurt child in here.

- **Chamber 2**: Impotence literally means powerlessness. If you feel powerless in any area of your relationship, this may result in impotence, whether you are a man or a woman. And there is a stuck youngster in here who needs you to empower them.

- **Chamber 3**: If you feel emotionally needy, or feel you cannot get the love and attention you need, there is an infant in here still looking for nurturing.

- **Chamber 4**: This chamber is about self-love, where you are more interested in getting your love needs met than opening your heart to your partner. The lesson here is to overcome selfishness and self-centredness.

- **Chamber 5**: In this chamber, you seek the gratification of a sensation rather than an expression of love.

When you have learned these five lessons, you move on. It is possible, though, to continue your journey but still have stuck energy in a particular chamber.

In the next three chambers, the lessons are about balancing your emotional needs:

- **Chamber 6**: Here you offer emotional comfort to others because this is what you need yourself. You may give your all in a relationship in the hope of getting it reciprocated. You are warm and loving, but underlying it is your neediness. Emotional rescuers are stuck here.

- **Chamber 7**: This is a transitional chamber. It moves you from nurturing someone else in order to get something back to being able to nurture genuinely with love.

- **Chamber 8**: This too is a transitional chamber, as you move from insecurity about your sexuality (and possibly shutting it down or expressing it inappropriately) to a sense of security, self-acceptance and assurance. This is particularly important now, as genders are becoming more fluid in preparation for the Golden Age.

When you have mastered the lessons of the first eight chambers, the frequency of your sacral will rise as you become more genuinely kind and loving, nurture your friendships and care for others. You are now moving to the higher lessons:

- **Chamber 9**: When you have progressed this far through your sacral, it starts to ascend and begins to glow. This chamber radiates caring, tenderness and nurturing so that you attract people who know how to love. You care for each other and this enriches your friendships as well as your partnerships.

- **Chamber 10**: You become more sensitive, warm, compassionate and tender in your relationships.

- **Chamber 11**: You reach out with love to others.

- **Chamber 12**: Now you are genuinely able to give love without holding back or expecting anything in return.

- **Chamber 13**: You share love. You give and receive in equal measure.

- **Chamber 14**: You express transcendent sexuality and pure love.

- **Chamber 15**: Your purpose in the physical act of sex is to bring in a soul. If you do not have children or you have unintentionally conceived, you may have learned this lesson in another life.

- **Chamber 16**: This experience is about carrying a baby with love or being part of an extended network that is lovingly supporting the pregnant person. Again, you may have done this in another life.

- **The 33rd chamber**, encapsulating the sacral and navel, is clairsentience, where you tune in to the emotions of others.

In the Golden Era of Atlantis, some people became androgynous when they had mastered all the lessons in the sacral chakra. At that time, this centre was only about expressing pure spiritual love, so people only had sex if they wanted to have a child. This is inconceivable to most people now, but it is part of the fifth-dimensional blueprint of the golden future.

VISUALIZATION TO HEAL THE SACRAL CHAKRA

- Find a place where you can be quiet and undisturbed.

- Close your eyes, breathe comfortably and let yourself relax.

- Be aware of a pure white light as Archangel Gabriel stands in front of you, ready to support you.

- Sense any cords in your sacral chakra from this and every other lifetime. It may be full of them, or there may be just a few. Without judgement, carefully cut them away.

- Then gently pull them all out by the roots and place them in a pile.

- Archangel Gabriel is calling in his fire dragons. Be aware of an army of pure white dragons, like glinting diamonds, approaching, breathing fire.

- They swirl round you, burning up and transmuting all the cords and any lower energies round you.

- See yourself lovingly holding hands with members of your family and partners past and present.

- Sense your sacral chakra glowing soft luminous pink.

Chapter 27

Embracing Oneness

Oneness unites us with all life-forms and with the Infinite. It recognizes that there is no them and us, only one, and is a key to higher ascension.

This quality is the lesson of the glorious, extraordinary and powerful navel chakra.

The navel chakra

From this chakra, you radiate warmth, welcome, friendship, self-worth and togetherness. In the Golden Era of Atlantis, it was the special energy from this chakra that enabled the people of that civilization to embrace the divine in all beings. They communed as one and greeted one another at a soul level.

> *As the navel chakra is being established once more,*
> *oneness consciousness will return to Earth. We*
> *will live in warm, welcoming communities.*

Planetary and cosmic navel chakras

The planetary navel chakra is Fiji, located approximately 3,000 miles from the planetary sacral chakra in Honolulu, both in the South Pacific.

The cosmic navel is the Sun. When your personal chakra is glowing orange, it connects directly with the Sun, and beyond that to Helios, the Great Central Sun. Helios is a stargate, a vast gateway to Source. When it opens, Source energy flows down into Helios, then into the Sun, where the frequency is stepped down before it is beamed into Fiji and spread round the world.

In Helios, Archangel Metatron is taking the current consciousness of humanity and alchemizing it into something far beyond our comprehension, creating the high-frequency light matter out of which the new will emerge for the new Golden Age. If I think of an egg, I find the divine alchemy that transforms it into a chick awesome beyond imagining. What Archangel Metatron is creating for us is as great a metamorphosis.

Archangel Metatron is also creating the light Codes of Oneness as well as the Codes of Power that will be established in the navel chakras of humanity.

The Codes of Oneness

The Codes of Oneness
are already encoded within us.

They radiate the warm, welcoming energy that will enable us to embrace the divine in one another so that we relate at a soul level. We will communicate with one another's Higher Selves and connect with the illumined ones and angelic beings and once more see the entire universe through enlightened eyes.

When this happens, we will automatically draw in Christ Light at a ninth-dimensional frequency.

Christ Light will fill your navel with transcendent
love, wisdom, peace and protection.

The Codes of Power

The Sun carries the Codes of Power that hold the pure Divine Masculine light. This contains raw power and force, strength and courage, as well as masculine qualities including confidence, independence, logic, focus, discipline, assertiveness and inspired leadership. This beams into the navel chakra, igniting the Codes of Power that are contained within it, and renders it very powerful and effective, when used with responsibility.

However, towards the end of Atlantis, this power was misused. In fact it was the use of this chakra for personal gain that caused the fall of Atlantis. This is why the navel was one of the five chakras that was withdrawn at that time. It has taken 10,000 years for the frequency of humanity to rise enough so that we can be trusted once more to use it for the highest good.

- The power of the navel can be used to boost your courage to speak your truth with wisdom, so that you can become a bright spiritual light.

- It can empower you to take responsibility for leading many into the new Golden Age.

- It can help you with DNA reprogramming.

- It can help you to manifest your visions or your personal desires (this latter is what caused it to be withdrawn).

It is time for lightworkers to reinstate the special qualities of the navel as we approach the new Golden Age.

Archangel Gabriel

Archangel Gabriel is in charge of the development of both the sacral and navel chakras. As I explained earlier, these were separate centres during the Golden Era of Atlantis, and when the vibration of that civilization declined, the navel was withdrawn and the Codes of Oneness and Power were no longer available to us.

Now, the more deeply the Codes of Oneness are established within you, the warmer and more welcoming you become. When you live with acceptance, look for the best in others and are totally at peace and in harmony, this chakra becomes clear and radiates serenity.

As this happens, Archangel Gabriel works through you to activate your inventive, imaginative talents. You may never have painted before, but now you suddenly feel a desire to get out the paintbrushes. You may be consumed with longing to make pottery, embroider a tapestry or create something else that is beautiful.

When this chakra radiates love, Archangel
Gabriel helps you to bring out and express
your creative and artistic abilities.

The lessons of the navel chakra

Currently the navel contains 16 chambers or lessons, as does the sacral below it. These two are enclosed in a large chamber which forms the 33rd, which is clairsentience.

When we embrace the blueprint for the fully perfected human, the navel and sacral will once more separate to become incredible chakras in their own right. However, as with all spiritual centres, we go through a spiritual journey within each one. That of the navel is from separation all the way through to oneness.

As you read about and explore the first few lessons of this chakra, you may find your lost and lonely inner child, and this is your opportunity to reassure them of their worth and help them to feel safe. This is particularly so if you ever feel lonely. Loneliness has been a learning experience for the western world, especially since the Industrial Revolution.

Remember that Archangel Gabriel is always with you as you work with this centre and you may like to ask him to place a light in each chamber before you enter it.

- **Chamber 1**: You feel isolated from others and the world.

- **Chamber 2**: You withdraw from friends, family and others.

- **Chamber 3**: You are cold or detached, so that others perceive you as unreachable and aloof.

- **Chamber 4**: You either have very tight boundaries, because you are afraid of life and people, or you are totally unbounded, so that you do not know where you begin or others end.

- **Chamber 5**: You find it difficult to relate to others. You feel you don't fit in or belong.

If any of the above apply to you, reassure and comfort your inner child. Let your inner wise parents talk to you. Alternatively, call in ascended beings and listen as they tell you that you are unique and special and lovable exactly as you are.

- **Chamber 6**: By the time you reach this lesson, you are beginning to feel friendly, warm and nurturing towards everyone.

- **Chamber 7**: You reach out and welcome others.

- **Chamber 8**: You are warm, caring and understanding to everyone.

- **Chamber 9**: You serve others by nourishing them emotionally. Examples of this may be cooking a meal for them, running a bath for them, inviting them into your home. You are hospitable.

- **Chamber 10**: When this chamber is open, you see the best in others. You actively see their good qualities.

- **Chamber 11**: You are sociable and meet up with others.

- **Chamber 12**: Your family is important and you support its togetherness. You may do this, for example, by phoning individuals and keeping them in touch with family news, or hosting a tele-call with them all, providing an open house, holding family get-togethers, or in other ways.

- **Chamber 13**: You help to build and nurture community. Even simple things like picking up litter or chatting to your neighbours contribute to the light in this chamber.

- **Chamber 14**: You are inclusive and ensure everyone feels they belong. Wherever you are, you draw people in.

- **Chamber 15**: You organize or participate in communal celebrations where everyone has the opportunity to come together.

- **Chamber 16**: You listen without judgement and offer unconditional guidance and support.

- **The 33rd chamber**, encapsulating the sacral and navel, is clairsentience.

As more people become fifth-dimensional and accept the lessons of the navel, co-operative, loving communities are coming together. Cultures throughout the world understand and honour diversity. We will all lovingly see the richness and variety of the world's people.

When the navel expands, we are drawn to our divine missions and a spiritual support network forms around us.

The memory of the oneness experienced during Golden Atlantis is recorded within all our navel chakras. As the new Golden Age approaches, this part of our blueprint will be activated and help to bring us all together in unity. This will thrust humanity fully into the fifth dimension.

*At its highest expression, our navel is
about oneness and unity with the Infinite.
This is a key to higher ascension.*

VISUALIZATION FOR ONENESS

- Find a place where you can be quiet and undisturbed.

- Close your eyes and relax.

- Call in 11 golden Solar Dragons from Helios and sense them powering towards you.

- Sense them surround you, shimmering with golden light and radiating love.

- Ask them to burn up anything that separates you from others – any thoughts, beliefs, emotional scars or experiences from this lifetime or others.

- Know that they are spiralling round you, cleansing your energy fields, raising your frequency and clearing the world around you with their golden fire.

- See golden threads radiating from you and touching every single person and animal on the planet.

Chapter 28

Connecting to the Knowledge, Wisdom and Power of Earth

In the centre of our planet there is a vast seventh-dimensional chakra called Hollow Earth. It is huge beyond imagining and is a world within a world. Here, within a great pyramid, is stored the history, knowledge and wisdom of everything that has ever happened on this planet.

This includes information about the five Golden Ages that have preceded us: the Age of Angala, when this planet was birthed; the Golden Age of Africa, known as Petranium; the Ages of Mu and Lemuria, both in the Pacific; and finally the Age that has just ended, Atlantis.

Within Hollow Earth are also held the keys to the ancient cultures that have particularly impacted on our planet, the powers of the 12 most influential portals and their energies, and all the information about the animal, bird and ocean kingdoms, including the etheric counterpart of any creature that has ever incarnated on the planet. Encoded within Hollow Earth is all the known knowledge of the elemental, angelic and deva kingdoms, as well as the sacred mysteries of time and speed, other dimensions, stars, planets and galaxies, sacred geometry, light, sound, alchemy, oneness and much more.

Full information about the knowledge and wisdom held in Hollow Earth, including the sound and colour keys to access it, is available in *The Keys to the Universe*, a book that I co-wrote with Kathy Crosswell.

Access to all this Earth information, wisdom
and power is available to you through your
fifth-dimensional solar plexus chakra.

The solar plexus chakra

The solar plexus chakra is very sensitive. It governs your stomach, liver, spleen and intestines. Most people recognize that if you are tense when eating, you do not absorb the nourishment properly. This spiritual centre digests not only food, but also life experiences. It is the seat of instinct, gut feelings and reactions, and is an accurate guide for you. It helps you to discern the truth. This is really vital now during this time of massive disinformation.

This chakra can often quite suddenly draw to your conscious awareness changes that need to be made. For example, you may be insouciantly walking down the road and unexpectedly you receive a flash of knowing that it is time to move house or to leave a relationship.

Nudges from your Higher Self are
sent through your gut feelings.

Let your solar plexus tell you who and what you can
trust. It will guide you to what is right for you.

At a third-dimensional frequency, this chakra is yellow and constantly on the lookout for danger. It also absorbs the fears of those around you, especially those that plug into your own.

However, when your solar plexus is fully fifth-dimensional, it relaxes and radiates the light of golden wisdom. You feel tranquil, serene, calm and confident, trusting your angels and guides to look after you. Now your solar plexus chakra transmutes the fears of others without taking in their energy, and touches people, known and unknown, with peace.

When you have earned the right to access
true wisdom, your solar plexus becomes
deep gold with rainbow lights.

At this level, the beautiful high-frequency antennae of this chakra reach out, seeking higher spiritual perspectives on all situations at home and abroad and spreading peace to soothe them.

When you look for the good in people and situations,
your solar plexus chakra glows with Christ Light.
No one can influence you. You are a master.

Planetary and cosmic solar plexus chakras

The solar plexus of our planet is the whole of South Africa. For thousands of years this country has absorbed and transmuted the fears of the world and it needs us all to send it golden energy of peace, harmony and wisdom. This will then spread throughout Africa and the planet.

The solar plexus of the universe is our planet, Earth. For the past 260,000 years, while our universe has been fourth-dimensional, our planet has absorbed and transmuted all the fear arising in the cosmos. This has been a mighty undertaking and is one of the reasons Earth was overwhelmed by lower energy and became third-dimensional. Because of this, there is much goodwill towards us, and many spiritual hands reaching out from the universe to help us back into our rightful position in the great scheme of things.

Archangel Uriel

Archangel Uriel is in charge of the evolution of the solar plexus chakra of humanity. He radiates deep gold with ruby light. He sends light into you to heal your solar plexus, dissolving any shock and trauma that you may be holding on to by enfolding you in love. He can lift depression and help you to see the possibilities of your life. He beams light into you to help you heal any fear of death and pass over beautifully. He draws negativity from the chambers of the solar plexus chakra and pours in golden energy. Every time you choose peace over conflict, calm over aggression or courage over cowardice, you strengthen your solar plexus and Archangel Uriel connects more closely to you.

As your solar plexus evolves and your true self-worth is established, the wisdom of your soul comes forward, enabling you to access all you have learned in past lives. You can also tune in to the massive store of knowledge and wisdom of our planet that is held within Hollow Earth.

Archangel Uriel also directs the golden Angels of Peace who work through us to bring unity and calm to the world. As your solar plexus chakra becomes fifth-dimensional, you can become a true ambassador for peace in the world. When it is fully evolved, you can connect with other star systems to spread goodwill and enjoy a sense of total alignment with the universe.

The lessons of the solar plexus chakra

There is an exceptionally wide range of lessons in the solar plexus. They go from mastering fear and cowardice right up to bringing forward wisdom and stepping into intergalactic mastery. You may already have learned them all, but if you find that one chamber is dark or that there is a stuck part of yourself still there, ask Archangel Uriel to light it up.

The first 16 chambers hold some sort of fear that it is time to transmute. Fortunately, just reading, with an attitude of self-acceptance, about the energies and lessons we all have to learn often enables Archangel Uriel to pour in his wisdom! Remember to ask for this before you read.

- **Chamber 1**: In the first chamber you learn to master aggression or conflict. Suspend judgement of yourself and remember that almost everyone holds anger that has been suppressed for generations and lifetimes. It also arises from the fear held by your inner child that you are not good enough, or recognized, or are trapped, or cannot win, and many other fears. Take a moment to find the part of you that is angry and listen to it. Ask Archangel Uriel to light up this chamber with golden wisdom.

- **Chamber 2**: Cowardice. We are all afraid of something, from stepping into the unknown to change, pain, consequences, rejection and/or death. Here tests are given to you to see if you act with courage and bravery or are timid, weak and cowardly. When you have passed these tests, you feel stronger and safer and your light is brighter. Ask Archangel Uriel to strengthen you.

- **Chamber 3**: Fear of loss. In this chamber lies our human fear of loss. This may be of losing a friend, partner or child, or a job, home or car. Understanding that nothing is ever taken unless it is a soul agreement and for the highest good may help you to let go of attachments. Remember that losses can build up over lifetimes and ask Archangel Uriel to help you release them. Ask him to fill this chamber with golden peace.

- **Chamber 4**: When you feel anxious or insecure, you are facing the lessons of the fourth chamber and you are called on to overcome these fears and remain calm and centred. They arise from beliefs and imagination, and it can help to focus on positive pictures, then ask Archangel Uriel to light them up with gold.

- **Chamber 5:** Many people hold themselves back and draw difficult conditions to themselves by imagining the worst possible outcome. If there is part of you stuck in this chamber, actively visualize the best outcome for any situation in your life and do this regularly until it becomes a new habit.

- **Chamber 6:** Being a bully or a victim. These are opposite outcomes of the same belief. Both come from your inner child feeling inadequate, so if this chamber is dark, engage in positive self-talk and ask Archangel Uriel to support you.

- **Chamber 7:** When you are mentally or emotionally reliant or dependent on another, either for support or for their opinions, for example in a co-dependent relationship, energy is stuck in this chamber. So make yourself as self-reliant as possible, while being able to co-operate with others.

- **Chamber 8:** The lesson of this chamber is to build healthy self-esteem, in other words make your self-perception realistic and honest. There can be opposite extremes here. One is to inflate your picture of self. The converse is low self-esteem, where your self-talk is negative. If this is the case, place a higher value on yourself and believe you are deserving.

- **Chamber 9:** This chamber is about self-worth, which is the belief that you have innate worth as a human being.

- **Chamber 10:** Here you learn to have faith in yourself to do or say the right and appropriate thing. Build your confidence to ignite the light here.

- **Chamber 11:** Arrogance comes from a lack of self-esteem and worth. Let it go!

- **Chamber 12**: Lack of trust in people. If part of this chamber is dark, explore what happened to you as a child and reframe it. Then look at how you trust yourself.

- **Chamber 13**: Learn to have trust in life. Notice just how often people or the universe support you.

- **Chamber 14**: Fully let go of wariness and suspicion so that this light can glow. You can do this by looking for the best in others.

- **Chamber 15**: The ego wants to accomplish out of a desire to receive accolades. Here you let go of this and aim to accomplish out of a desire to be of service.

- **Chamber 16**: Here you let others influence you or feel they are better than you are. Stand in your power.

And now the chambers in your solar plexus start to glow with fifth-dimensional light. Moving on:

- **Chamber 17**: You accept yourself exactly as you are.

- **Chamber 18**: You stand up for the rights of others.

- **Chamber 19**: You trust others because you see the best in them. When you do this, you can rely on them.

- **Chamber 20**: Independence. This is where you stand in your power as a master.

- **Chamber 21**: Receiving love. Open yourself to the love of humans and animals. Archangel Uriel can also beam Source love into this chamber, so open the doors wide.

- **Chamber 22**: Trusting yourself. As you master all the lessons of this chakra, you fully trust your own intuition and decisions.

- **Chamber 23**: Humility. The lesson of this chamber is to have good self-worth so that you listen to others and pay attention to their needs and feelings.

- **Chamber 24**: Inner peace. You have cultivated a feeling of serenity and tranquillity that you maintain no matter what is happening around you.

- **Chamber 25**: Spreading peace. This chamber is so golden that it automatically radiates peace around you.

- **Chamber 26**: Empowering others. You actively bring others forward and enable them to feel good about themselves.

- **Chamber 27**: Sharing for the highest good. This is where people and communities become interdependent.

- **Chamber 28**: The lesson of this chamber is harmlessness, which is a highly evolved quality. When you develop it, all people and animals feel safe with you.

- **Chamber 29**: Healing your past lives. Set your intention to forgive yourself and others, then sense the thread of your lives going back through time and space. Ask Archangel Uriel to heal and transmute your timeline.

- **Chamber 30**: Wisdom, with the confidence it brings.

- **Chamber 31**: Bringing forward wisdom from your past lives. This chamber glows deep gold as past wisdom becomes available to you.

- **Chamber 32**: Connecting with intergalactic wisdom. Affirm that you are ready to receive downloads from beings of light.

- **Chamber 33**: Being an intergalactic master. You stand in your true power and worth, connected to All That Is.

VISUALIZATION FOR PEACE

- See or sense your solar plexus chakra radiating deep golden light.

- Take a moment to breathe into it.

- Visualize yourself kneeling in front of Archangel Uriel.

- He touches you with the Sword of Peace and intergalactic mastery.

- Sense yourself surrounded by his Angels of Peace.

- Direct them to spread peace round the world.

Chapter 29

Awakening Your Higher Heart

Your essence is love. It always has been and always will be. Love is the filament of a bulb that is white-hot perfect. Only dust and dirt on the glass dim the light. The white-hot centre is like the pure white centre of your fifth-dimensional heart that connects through the Cosmic Heart directly to Source. You can make the connection and see it clearly by cleaning the glass of the bulb.

This is done by seeing the divine love in the heart of every person and recognizing that everything else is ego.

The journey of the heart is from
self-centredness to pure love.

The heart chakra

There are 33 chambers in the heart chakra. The outer ones are green, where your heart is closed, and here you go through experiences and lessons of self-centredness. It helps to open the doors and place the flame of love within each room. However evolved you are, as with all the chakras, there may still be some lessons not yet fully mastered. As you open to love, you move inwards to pink chambers, then, as your love becomes more spiritual, to violet pink ones, until you reach the innermost pure white chambers of your higher heart.

The desire to find love is the force driving
every single situation or disagreement between
people. Now at last we can all find it.

Planetary and cosmic heart chakras

The heart chakra of our planet is in Glastonbury in the United Kingdom.

The heart chakra of the universe is the planet Venus. The portal from Glastonbury Tor to Venus was opened and activated by Jesus, who is now the Bringer of Cosmic Love. Thousands of people sense the love energy pouring through this portal and are drawn to Glastonbury to activate their own heart centres.

Venus, the Cosmic Heart, receives the frequencies of divine love directly from Source. These are shimmering white. The planet is a transformer that steps down this love to frequencies that we can accept. When you connect to the Cosmic Heart in meditation or sleep, it accelerates your journey to love.

Archangel Chamuel

Archangel Chamuel overlights the evolution and development of the heart chakra. He usually presents himself as pure white with a hint of soft pink. He beams to you the highest frequency of love that you can accept.

Spiritual beings that work with your heart centre

When you work with this chakra, it helps to invoke the following angelic beings:

- Your unicorn
- A beautiful pink dragon

- Archangel Chamuel, the Angel of the Heart

- Archangel Metatron, who is in charge of the entire ascension process and intimately connected with the opening of the heart

Before you read about the journey through your heart centre, ask them to focus their energy on it to light your way through the chambers. Here is an invocation to help you to draw them to you:

I now invoke a beautiful pink dragon to burn up any dense energies released from the lower chambers of my heart.

I invoke my beloved pure and beautiful unicorn to purify and illuminate all the chambers of my heart.

I invoke Archangel Chamuel to help me integrate any lessons I have not yet fully absorbed, so that my heart can accept pure love.

I invoke Archangel Metatron to turn the Metatron Cube anti-clockwise in front of each chamber to draw out any blocks remaining in it.

When this is complete, I ask Archangel Metatron to rotate the Metatron Cube clockwise to recode the chambers and to fill them with glorious sixth or seventh-dimensional light.

So be it.

Trust that this is now happening in divine right order and your unicorn, Archangel Chamuel, Archangel Metatron and a luminous pink dragon are focusing their energy on this chakra as it ascends.

The journey through the heart

The human heart centre grows and evolves over lifetimes. Be prepared to examine yourself as you go through the steps towards pure love and take this opportunity to clear, release and forgive anything you are holding on to. Enter the first chamber holding your flame of love.

- **Chamber 1**: Here you explore any acts of unkindness you have committed or maybe are still committing. Forgive yourself for the past and resolve to be kind at all times.

- **Chamber 2**: When your heart is shut down, you are unfeeling or cold, so light it up and open the doors and windows to love.

- **Chamber 3**: In this chamber you nurse your feelings of hurt or anger. These may have spoiled a relationship or another aspect of your life in some way. Ask yourself how long you are prepared to blemish your incarnation by holding on to past feelings.

- **Chamber 4**: The green-eyed monster, jealousy, means that you don't feel lovable enough. If there is green slime in this chamber, clear it out and open your heart.

- **Chamber 5**: When you are self-absorbed you cannot reach out to others, this chamber is closed. Throw open the doors and take an interest in other people.

- **Chamber 6**: Here is held the fear that there is not enough for you, so you are greedy. Start to give things away and watch how more flows back to you.

- **Chamber 7**: Here you withdraw into yourself. If you recognize this, make a big effort to take off your armour and let others in.

- **Chamber 8**: When you experience loneliness, energy is stuck in this chamber. Be warm and friendly and you will attract people on your wavelength.

- **Chamber 9**: When you withhold yourself or things, or you are mean, the door of this chamber remains shut, for you are blocking the flow of life. Recognize this and consciously let every area of your life flow.

- **Chamber 10**: This is the last of the lower chambers. Here you are sad or unhappy. If this is the case, connect to nature and receive its healing.

Now the petals start to open.

- **Chamber 11**: You feel and express love for animals.

- **Chamber 12**: You love nature.

- **Chamber 13**: You feel and express love for children.

- **Chamber 14**: You feel and express love for your partner.

- **Chamber 15**: You feel and express love for your family or someone else's.

- **Chamber 16**: You feel and express love for others.

- **Chamber 17**: You love yourself, who you truly are.

- **Chamber 18**: You empathize with others.

- **Chamber 19**: You feel compassion for others.

- **Chamber 20**: You care for other people.

- **Chamber 21**: You forgive others.

- **Chamber 22**: You forgive the entire Earth experience, all you have ever done or felt and all that has been done to you, as well as human inhumanity.

- **Chamber 23**: You forgive yourself.

- **Chamber 24**: You are warm-hearted.

- **Chamber 25**: You are welcoming and hospitable.

- **Chamber 26**: You are generous.

- **Chamber 27**: You give without conditions.

- **Chamber 28**: You have love for the whole of humanity.

- **Chamber 29**: You feel and offer unconditional love.

- **Chamber 30**: You move into transcendent love.

- **Chamber 31**: You connect with the Cosmic Heart.

- **Chamber 32**: You experience cosmic love.

- **Chamber 33**: This is true oneness.

When you live from your higher heart, you glow with love and everyone feels good in your presence. Your light affects the cosmos.

VISUALIZATION TO REACH THE HIGHER HEART

- Affirm that you forgive everyone and every situation that is not love.

- Sense or see Archangel Chamuel standing in front of you.

- His hands are on your heart chakra.

- Pure love is pouring directly into your heart.

- All you can see or sense or feel is love.

- Breathe into your heart.

- Feel it radiating pure love into the world.

Chapter 30

Staying True to Yourself

In fifth-dimensional consciousness, you automatically speak your truth. When everyone around you is clairvoyant and can see your energies, there is no point in being anything other than open and honest! At this frequency, you are honourable, courageous and strong, and have the highest integrity. These qualities are vital for mastery and we are called on to practise them now, in preparation for the new Golden Age. When all the people in the world live at this level of honour, there will be total trust and safety.

The journey to truth

In the throat chakra, there are 22 chambers or lessons that guide you on the path to honour and courage. As you explore these lessons, your aura becomes clear and honest, and you open up to spiritual gifts, including healing, until you have total faith in God. This is the chakra of higher communication.

There has been a development over the last few years, as the throat centre has expanded and incorporated the Alta Major chakra, with its 11 chambers, making 33 lessons, in line with so many other chakras.

The Alta Major chakra

I first heard of the Alta Major chakra nearly 40 years ago at a talk by Ruth White, who channels Gildas. No one had heard of this chakra before and the people who were facilitating the event were sceptical, demanding to know why no one knew of it. Clearly, as the ascension of humanity was then in its very early stages, it had not been evident or available before, and Ruth brought the information through.

The Alta Major chakra is situated at the base of the skull, where it joins the neck. When you are third-dimensional, it contains much of the programming that plugs you into the illusion of the old matrix. As you wake up spiritually, these old beliefs have to be cleared, which is rather like wiping a computer disk so that entirely new information can be downloaded. However, it is not as easy as wiping a computer disk, because many people, religions, governments and others are keen to maintain the status quo. Courage is often needed in order to let go of illusion and fully wake up to the truth of your divinity.

The Alta Major is often called the Seat of Consciousness, and connects with the Seat of the Soul in the base chakra. It used to be considered a minor ascension chakra, but as the old is being dissolved and it is becoming fifth-dimensional, it is proving to be glorious.

The fifth-dimensional Alta Major provides the missing 11 chambers or lessons of the higher throat and takes the lessons here to an entirely new level.

All those years ago, Ruth White described it as brown. As with all the chakras, the colour frequency has evolved and now it is deep blue-green or teal.

Blue brings truth, strength, protection, healing and peace, while green is the colour of nature, growth and new beginnings. This particular vibration of teal is one of the new colours being brought through to help the ascension of humanity.

*The Alta Major aspect of the throat is a junction
point and is energetically linked to the higher heart.
It also connects the crown, third eye and base by
activating the kundalini to flow more freely.*

Planetary and cosmic throat chakras

The throat chakra of Earth is Luxor in Egypt. The cosmic throat is Mercury, which is about communication, and the part of Mercury that has already ascended is known as Telephony.

Archangel Michael

Archangel Michael vibrates on a deep blue level, reflecting the highest aspects of the throat chakra and the blue within the teal of the Alta Major section. He carries his Sword of Truth to cut away lower energies, and his angels will always protect you if you ask. He is always with you as you work on your higher throat.

The journey through the higher throat chakra

The journey through the throat centre has 22 steps and the Alta Major 11. In total this is 33, the vibration of Christ consciousness.

All the throat chambers are exceptionally sensitive, so you need extra protection as you take your journey through them.

This is a journey to higher consciousness and you are asked to start with the inner chambers and work outwards round the spiral, so that the most delicate energies in its vulnerable centre are safeguarded.

In addition, before you start to read and integrate the lessons of this centre, pause for a moment to ask Archangel Michael, as well as a deep blue dragon and your unicorn, to protect your exploration and hold the frequency for you, with the words:

I now invoke Archangel Michael to place your deep blue light of protection around me during this journey, a deep blue dragon to clear my path and protect me, and a pure white unicorn to hold my frequency high.

As with all the chakras, you may have undertaken some of the journey in past lives.

- **Chamber 33**: The knowing of cosmic oneness. You may have experienced this knowing while looking at the stars on a tranquil evening.

- **Chamber 32**: The feeling of oneness is expanded to include oneness with nature and the cosmos.

- **Chamber 31**: You bring the energy of the Cosmic Heart into this chamber. Take a moment to do this consciously.

- **Chamber 30**: You access higher codes to ascension. Archangel Michael will download these if you ask and if you are ready.

- **Chamber 29**: You gain completely fresh perspectives on life and mastery.

- **Chamber 28**: You connect with higher beings – angels, masters and highly evolved beings from other star or planetary systems.

- **Chamber 27**: You remember important details of your soul's journey. You may find yourself bringing forward wisdom as well as knowledge.

- **Chamber 26**: You remember significant events of your past lives.

- **Chamber 25**: You fully heal your past lives. This is about deeper forgiveness.

- **Chamber 24**: You trust your intuition to the extent that you verbalize it.

- **Chamber 23**: You download inspired concepts in order to share them.

- **Chamber 22**: You have absolute and total trust in God.

- **Chamber 21**: You learn to have trust in yourself.

- **Chamber 20**: You are an ambassador of light and hold the Flame of Truth for this purpose.

- **Chamber 19**: You exercise inspired leadership with integrity.

- **Chamber 18**: You recognize who you truly are and honour your divine magnificence.

- **Chamber 17**: You teach truths telepathically and verbally.

- **Chamber 16**: You always speak with honour and integrity.

- **Chamber 15**: You are open and aligned to higher truth.

- **Chamber 14**: You are able to speak up for yourself.

- **Chamber 13**: You can and do speak up for others.

- **Chamber 12**: You know who you are.

- **Chamber 11**: You accept your true magnificence.

- **Chamber 10**: When you speak, you actively empower others.

- **Chamber 9**: You communicate telepathically.

- **Chamber 8**: You speak the divine truth, no matter what others say or do.

And now look at the lower lessons of this chakra and take the opportunity to release these fears:

- **Chamber 7:** You go along with the opinions of others and allow yourself to be influenced to misrepresent the truth. If you realize this is the case, stop and decide what is right for you.

- **Chamber 6:** You hold back for fear of being misunderstood, disbelieved or persecuted. These are beliefs from childhood or past lives. It is time to claim your power and radiate your truth.

- **Chamber 5:** You are learning to trust your inner voice and the promptings of your guardian angel.

- **Chamber 4:** The lesson here is to listen and really hear so that you comprehend the message.

- **Chamber 3:** In this chamber you are refusing to listen. If you believe this is the case, sit down quietly each day and be receptive. You may not receive guidance or impressions immediately, but if you persist, you will. Then the light will shine in this chamber.

- **Chamber 2:** You deliberately tell falsehoods or distort the truth. This is either a manipulation or a protection of your inner child. It is time consciously to let it go.

- **Chamber 1:** You lie or are dishonest to protect yourself. Change this, for when you speak your truth, this chamber lights up, this is reflected throughout your aura and people will start to respect and trust you.

Your throat chakra is now radiating shimmering translucent deep blue with a hint of green. Everyone sees you as honourable and trusts you.

VISUALIZATION FOR ARCHANGEL
MICHAEL'S SWORD OF TRUTH

- Call in a deep blue dragon to create a vortex of protective blue energy round you.

- Ask your unicorn to stand by you and hold your frequency high.

- Ask Archangel Michael to touch you with honour, integrity and truth.

- Take a moment to feel and acknowledge these energies.

- Archangel Michael gently touches your throat with his flaming Sword of Truth.

- Sense old stuff and patterns that hold you back being cut away.

- You may sense a pure blue flame light up, filling your throat centre.

- See yourself speaking your truth.

- Feel a surge of energy as the blue flame expands and surrounds your body.

Chapter 31

Activating Your Spiritual and Psychic Gifts

Some seers, wise ones with advanced spiritual and psychic abilities, can look into a crystal ball and see all that they need to know, past, present and future. When you are fully fifth-dimensional, your third eye chakra, in the centre of your forehead, becomes your own personal crystal ball.

The third eye chakra

There are 96 chambers in this complex and powerful chakra, and each one contains a lesson. We are not going through all those lessons here! However, this chakra is arranged on seven levels, and we will look at these.

It is a little like exploring a seven-storey apartment block. You may have visited some of the apartments on each floor, yet there are others that you have not explored. You may have integrated some of the knowledge, either in past incarnations or earlier in this one. You may be more psychic than you realize, without being fully telepathic or clairvoyant. In the same way, you may be receiving cosmic downloads, without enjoying abundance consciousness.

This is a very potent chakra and its power can be misused for personal gain or control, or be focused on the highest good. In the former case, it holds back your ascension and that of the planet. In the latter, you become a beacon of light and have a massive influence on the ascension of Earth.

Planetary and cosmic third eye chakras

The planetary third eye chakra is Afghanistan. Your third eye is powerful. So too are the mountains of Afghanistan, with their rich copper, gold, gemstones, oil and minerals.

This country is forecast to be the last place on the planet to be at peace. It reflects the third eye chakras of humanity, and the quicker we all ignite the light in this centre, the sooner we can enjoy world peace.

The third eye of the cosmos is Jupiter, the ascended aspect of which is called Jumbay. There is a portal from Afghanistan to Jupiter and Jumbay, so when that country rises into the fifth dimension, not only will there be peace on Earth, but happiness and abundance will spread to the entire planet.

Archangel Raphael

Archangel Raphael, the emerald-green Angel of Healing and Abundance, oversees the development of the third eye chakras of humanity, the planet and the universe. His twin flame is the Angel Mary, the wondrous healer who carries all the Divine Feminine qualities, especially love and compassion.

The seven levels of the third eye chakra

There are seven levels within this centre and each of these needs to be fully mastered and used for the benefit of all on your journey to higher ascension.

1. Illusion

The first level is about seeing through illusion to truth. Anything that is not of love and purest light is illusion. Disinformation and conspiracy theories abound now. What a perfect opportunity to discriminate between truth and illusion! I am a Virgo, and one of the big lessons of all Virgos is discernment and discrimination, so I have spent years working on this! I understand the excitement and drama of some of the theories, but I am learning to ignore all that is not truth. So much dark stuff, ranging from war to disease to divorce, seems very real, and feels very painful, especially when you are living through it. How can it possibly be an illusion?

Source is Love and Divine Light. This is truth. You are part of Source, so Love and Divine Light are your essence and that of every human and every animal in the world. Love in this case is defined as 'total acceptance without agenda or judgement' and Divine Light is the highest frequency of spiritual knowledge and information. If that is what you see in someone, or even the most dangerous animal, they will respond to you from the love in their pure essence.

It is only when you step away from the
blazing heart of Source that you see
through the distorted lens of illusion.

If you see anything that is not love or pure light, it is a projection of something within yourself. It must be so, for if it were not within you, you simply would not see it.

So the universe keeps providing you with mirrors to look into, so that you see unconscious aspects of yourself reflected in the people and situations around you. The more you focus on them and energize them, the more real they seem to be. I often receive frantic communications from people who want their partner, child, parent, colleague or friend to change. 'How can I get him to stop treating me that way?' 'How can I help her see she should move?' 'What can I do about my child's behaviour?' The answer is always the same: 'The other person is reflecting something back to you. Change yourself and the reflection must change, so they will behave differently or will leave your life.'

In addition, the other person's qualities or behaviours that you are focusing on are illusions. The truth is that hidden underneath is a beautiful divine being. Focus on their beautiful divine aspect so that they can show it to you.

Fear and ego are also illusions. The truth is that whatever your challenges, your spirit will come through it. Your ego may be dented, however, and that is a learning process on the journey to love.

If anyone tries to make you feel different from or
less than others, remember that is their illusion.

However, if you buy into it, it becomes yours. Just focus on the loving essence of who you are. If someone infers you are not as good as someone else, once again it is a test. When you disregard it and concentrate on your divine magnificence, you move beyond the first level of the third eye journey.

Several people may be looking into the same mirror and seeing the same thing. It doesn't matter how many people see the negative stuff, it is still an illusion. The collective can be very powerful. Much of the media buys into it and tests you in many ways. If anyone talks to you of war, hurt, or disagreement, they are focused on illusion.

Change the subject or the TV channel. Do not enter their universe. It is time for lightworkers to move beyond it.

You energize what you focus on, so
see the good and beautiful.

The ultimate illusion is death. The truth is that you are taking off the robes of your physical body in a changing room before emerging into the next room.

We have all heard people saying that the world is illusion. In the third dimension, we have individually and collectively co-created that drama. But it is impossible to understand until we step into pure love and light. Only then can we see and understand that it arises from separation from Source.

The moment you flick on the switch and truly recognize the negative film projected from your mind for what it is, at that instant you can choose to project a different film. The reflections change to joy and love. Your world transforms. While other people live in the dark, you do not need to join them.

In the fifth-dimensional paradigm
that we are approaching, we will all
step into light, love and truth.

If you want to transform the world ready for
the new Golden Age, you can start by making
the switch in your own consciousness. Then you
can move to the second level of the third eye.

2. Mental healing

The thoughts that you send out can affect others greatly. The more energy there is behind a thought, the more deeply it can penetrate the recipient's aura and affect their health and wellbeing, negatively or positively. However, most people's thoughts are too scattered to be effective.

The lessons in the second level of the third eye are about working with the power of your thoughts for healing and the highest good of others.

The current focus on meditation and mindfulness is all about developing this level of the third eye.

When you have the mental focus to send out a laser beam of concentrated positive thought with integrity and positive intent, you have mastered the lessons of this level. This confers such great power that you can use it to accelerate the ascension of the entire planet.

You can concentrate your power to visualize everyone's fifth-dimensional health blueprint in place. When you do this, ask that they receive this under grace. This means that you are asking that they benefit only if their soul agrees to accept it.

You can use your power to force something to happen, but if it is not for that person's highest good, you create karma for yourself. Asking under grace means that their soul guides the energy.

3. Telepathy

This is the ability to communicate directly from mind to mind without speech. Communications may arrive as pictures, words, thoughts, ideas, feelings or concepts.

More and more people are becoming telepathic without even realizing it. Most mothers communicate in this way with their babies and small children, though when the infant is screaming, arousing anxiety in the parent, this blocks the receptivity. In the same way, animal lovers are telepathic with their pets and intuitively know what they want. It is a two-way process, for the creature receives your thoughts, often more easily than your words. Again, if you try too hard, though, it clouds your third eye. It is much easier to open up to the airwaves when you are relaxed.

People or animals communicate on different frequency bands from birds or trees, while the angelic and elemental realms send their messages at a higher vibration. Yet your third eye can download them all.

Practise tuning in to people and animals as well as the nature and angelic kingdoms. Let go of any preconceptions and trust your impressions.

4. Creation

The fourth level of your third eye is about creation and manifestation. When your 12 fifth-dimensional chakras are engaged, you can manifest with the power of other chakras, but until recently the third eye was the only spiritual centre from which you could send your desires and intentions out into the universe. From here you can consciously manifest not only your personal dreams and visions, but also objects. Everyone has this latent power, which is developed and honed on this level of the third eye.

Manifestation is based on three factors:

- The ability to relax deeply

- Clear, concentrated focus on what you wish to create

- Raising your frequency as high as possible

Breathwork and relaxation techniques are becoming accepted as we start unconsciously to train ourselves to relax more deeply.

In the golden future, people will play memory games to sharpen their recall and also to improve their focus and concentration. Note how crosswords, sudoku and word games have become popular over the last few years.

From this level, you can also send pictures into the relaxed mind of someone who is receptive. I have shared the following story in another of my books, but it illustrates this beautifully. Forty years ago, I was training to be a hypnotherapist. One of my fellow students was practising on a friend. While the friend was deeply relaxed, this student took her on an inner journey along a pathway. She decided to project a pink stile into the mind of her friend. Suddenly the subject exclaimed, 'How extraordinary! A pink stile has appeared on the path.' This is something you can practise to bring forward your skills. It must be done with integrity.

5. Clairvoyance

The fifth level of your third eye is clairvoyance, the ability to see into other dimensions. While it literally means 'clear seeing', at this level you may be very aware and psychically attuned without actually being able to see pictures. You may, for example, merely have a strong sense of what will happen in the future or what has occurred in the past.

As with all gifts, it is vital to use this for the highest good, for there are dark dimensions that you can tune in to, with unfortunate consequences. The doors to those lower spaces are locked if you have pure intentions and thoughts. Only your own fears or choices, for example watching a dark television programme, can open them.

As you focus on higher realms and ascension qualities, the veils between you and the spiritual world become thinner. You may see spirits or even ascended masters as well as elementals, dragons, angels and unicorns.

6. Abundance consciousness

The sixth level of the third eye is about abundance consciousness. The chambers here start to open when you become fifth-dimensional. Then your needs are automatically met.

This can happen in subtle ways. For example, you're in a restaurant and think, *I'd like some tomato sauce*, and the waiter is instantly at your side, saying, 'Would you like some tomato sauce?' Or one morning you say, 'I need to change my car. I'd really like a blue Peugeot.' That afternoon you walk past your local garage and there is a blue Peugeot, on special offer. A friend of mine once said that he really needed a holiday. His phone rang five minutes later. It was a friend he hadn't seen for years inviting him to stay as his guest at his villa in France.

At this level, you believe you deserve these good things and are joyfully grateful for them. Then more miracles of abundance and prosperity happen as a matter of course. The universe sees your heart's desire and brings it to you.

Be ready to accept divine abundance.

7. Claircogniscence

The seventh level of the third eye is claircogniscence, divine knowing or *gnosis*.

This is the top floor of the seven-storey apartment block and from here you have a panoramic view. Things fall into place. You receive downloads from the stars. You access universal truths. You do not need to *see*. You *know*.

VISUALIZATION TO EXPAND YOUR THIRD EYE

- Imagine you are walking towards a seven-storey apartment block.

- Walk into the hall on the ground floor and look for beauty in each room.

- As you move from floor to floor, open the doors and let the sun shine into each room.

- On the second floor, focus on the world being healed.

- On the third floor, send a powerful and beautiful picture into someone's mind.

- On the fourth floor, focus on a dream or vision.

- On the fifth floor, look into the rooms and see what is happening in the different dimensions.

- On the sixth floor, imagine you are receiving your heart's desire from the universe.

- On the roof of the building, look up at the stars and feel a crystal ball being placed in your third eye.

Chapter 32

Connecting to the Cosmos

The cosmos is vast, full of stars, planets and galaxies. Billions of non-physical beings of all shapes and sizes inhabit the universes. While our entire universe will be fifth-dimensional by 2032, some of the celestial bodies and extraterrestrial beings in the cosmos have already evolved to even higher spiritual levels. All are focused on helping Earth take its rightful fifth-dimensional place in this universe.

The crown chakra

Your crown chakra, at the top of your head, has 1,000 petals. Each one reaches out into the universe to connect you to 1,000 stars, planets, galaxies or pools of cosmic energy.

When your crown chakra is fully fifth-dimensional, you radiate a golden halo, which people may even be able to see.

Archangel Jophiel

Archangel Jophiel is in charge of the development of the crown chakra to enable you to draw in cosmic knowledge, information and wisdom. This is downloaded into the chambers of the crown and usually arrives as total knowing. There is no doubt. You simply accept it all.

Cosmic helpers

Here are some of the cosmic beings who want to help us now. Be receptive to them and ask for their assistance, as they cannot contravene your free will.

- The beings from Sirius bring spiritual technology and an understanding of sacred geometry. The Golden Globe of ninth-dimensional Christ Light has recently been placed here. The ascended aspect of Sirius is Lakumay, which now holds the Golden Globe of 11th-dimensional Christ Light. Together, they beam high frequencies of transcendent love to you, if you are open to accepting it. You can also visit in your spiritual bodies to access it, when you are ready.

- Source heart healing is stepped down through the Pleiades. All the seventh-dimensional beings from this constellation carry blue heart-healing light in their energy fields, and they enfold you in this when you request it.

- The beings from Arcturus are highly evolved and are almost a group consciousness, where the good of all is more important than individual identity. These awesome beings are advanced healers, and they will work with your chakras, meridian lines, energy bodies and DNA if you request it.

- Venus has fully ascended and steps Source love down to a level we can accept. The beautiful beings from this planet can touch you with pure love, if you ask for it, and connect you to the Cosmic Heart.

- The beings from Andromeda are very highly evolved. They spread higher love, and as you too progress, you can step beyond the Cosmic Heart to receive extraordinary love from them. By drawing wisdom from Orion and peace from Nigellay, the ascended part of Mars, into their energy fields, they can truly raise your frequency.

- Neptune is the planet of higher spirituality. The wisdom and knowledge of both Lemuria and Atlantis is held in the part of it that has ascended, called Toutillay. Many of those who step their energy down through here carry the original blueprints with which they were blessed by Source. The beings from this planet touch you with divine purity and wisdom.

- Saturn is the planet of discipline and order. The spiritual laws of the universe are held here. Its ascended aspect is called Quichy. It is only with self-discipline that you can become a master or develop true power with wisdom. The beings from Saturn are endeavouring to touch you with these higher possibilities.

- Beings from Lyra are arriving now that the great stargate between this constellation and the Moon is opening. They are coming to prepare you for unicorn energy, while the beings from the Moon carry the codes of Divine Feminine wisdom and love, which they whisper to you, especially at full Moons.

- The beings from the Sun carry the codes of Divine Masculine energy and happiness, and will pass them on to you.

- The Sun beyond our Sun is called Helios, known as the Great Central Sun. Here, Archangel Metatron creates and holds all the light codes for this universe. The beings from here are touching those who are ready with the codes of the Divine Masculine as well as universal knowledge and wisdom.

- The beings from Mercury and its ascended part, Telephony, are attuned to the higher cosmic communication networks and are prepared to help you to connect to higher transmissions with integrity.

- The beings from Jupiter bring abundance consciousness, while those from its ascended aspect, Jumbay, enable you to expand all your spiritual concepts and fulfil your potential.

- The beings from Uranus and its ascended aspect, Curonay, are helping you to connect to the wisdom of all the stars, planets and galaxies from which you are ready to download information.

- The masters of Orion hold the wisdom of the universe. The beings from that constellation help you to use knowledge for the highest good of all.

- While Martians have the reputation of being aggressive, they are actually helping, with respect and honour, to keep the universe in divine order. The beings from the part of Mars that has ascended, Nigellay, pass on to you the qualities of the spiritual warrior. They are protectors, and wise and powerful leaders. They whisper to you to do your part to connect all beings of the universe with love.

VISUALIZATION TO OPEN UP
TO COSMIC WISDOM

- Focus on your crown chakra and imagine you are wearing a crown with 1,000 spikes or feelers reaching upwards.

- You may have a sense of one or more of these linking to stars, planets or cosmic energies.

- Allow yourself to receive knowledge and wisdom for the highest good.

- Pause as this is integrated consciously or unconsciously into your crown chakra.

- See the entire universe connected by love.

- Visualize a golden halo surrounding your crown chakra.

Chapter 33

Eternal Peace

Pure white contains the whole colour spectrum. It radiates purity. It is also the colour of Source love and eternal peace.

You have to earn the qualities that create pure white light in your energy fields. When you do, you are at such a level of peace that you are totally harmless, so people and animals around you feel completely relaxed and safe.

Eternal peace means that you live permanently in this benign state. If you were to walk through scrubland full of hungry lions, you would be untouched. When you live in pure white innocence, you are literally in your divine essence, which is a very advanced frequency.

There are two Angels of Peace, Archangel Uriel, who spreads peace with wisdom and harmony on the golden ray, and Archangel Christiel, who radiates peace on the pure white ray of love and joy.

The causal chakra

Your causal chakra lies above your crown and is known as your own personal moon, for it is shimmering white and holds Divine Feminine light. It is also connected directly to the Moon. It is the chakra of the higher mind and holds the consciousness of stillness, peace, love, joy and truth.

This spiritual centre is one huge single chamber. You gain access to it when you have developed the appropriate qualities. It is the gateway to the angelic realms. When this chakra is activated, its pearl-studded gates swing open and you may enter the seventh heaven, or seventh-dimensional world of the angels, unicorns and higher spiritual beings. You then step into the wondrous world of angels and archangels who connect with you and offer help when you need it. When you remember to ask, their assistance is readily and obviously available.

You can also connect even more closely to your guardian angel, who is constantly guiding you and also co-ordinating the synchronicities that enable you to meet the people and situations of your destiny.

You may even start to discern the different vibrations of the archangels as you link to them on a daily basis.

When your causal chakra is in place, you also begin to connect to unicorns, known as 'the purest of the pure'. They are often seen as pure white etheric horses with a spiralling horn of light. Like all beings of the angelic realms, they can take any shape or appear in any colour, but their essence is divine purity.

Many unicorns enter the energy fields of Earth by leaving Lyra and transiting via the Moon into the causal chakras of humans and through the gateway into the angelic realm round Earth. Millions of unicorns have connected to our planet and humanity in this way.

When you develop spiritually, there are so many ways of serving the world without even realizing you are doing so. Opening your causal chakra is one of them.

Planetary and cosmic causal chakras

The causal chakra of our planet is Tibet, that country of stillness, wisdom and peace. The High Priest Zeus led his tribe there, taking with him the energies of true peace, and these were eventually developed into the Buddhist religion. The great cosmic pyramid built here by Zeus and overseen by Archangel Christiel after the fall of Atlantis has been destroyed physically, but energetically it holds the keys and codes of peace on Earth.

This pyramid offers one of the entry points to the Halls of Amenti, within Hollow Earth, which are a vast library containing the records of all the spiritual achievements of the masters throughout the cosmos. It is protected by the Sentinels of Anubis.

The cosmic causal chakra is the Moon, and this is connected to the diamond-white cross-shaped stargate of Lyra, beyond which is the unicorn realm.

Archangel Christiel

Archangel Christiel is in charge of the development of this transcendent chakra. Like many other universal beings, he has only recently stepped down once more into this universe to assist the current transformation, and particularly to help Earth. His entry point is the stargate of Lyra that is the gateway to the unicorn kingdom. He radiates pure white and, as his name suggests, carries the highest frequencies of Christ Light. His etheric retreat above Earth is Jerusalem, and that of his twin flame, Archangel Mallory, is above Bethlehem.

He also accesses our planet through the Moon. When you think of Archangel Christiel while looking at the full Moon, or even thinking about it, his energy and that of the unicorns lights up your causal. It also enables angels to connect with you more easily. At these times, Archangel Christiel can download light keys and codes to you that can help to repattern the etheric DNA in your causal. These eventually filter into the physical and can affect you deeply.

Peace dragons

Dragons are fully of the angelic realms. Their wings demonstrate that their hearts are wide open. While some do not vibrate at a level where they can live in the seventh heaven, some of them do.

Among these are the silver lunar dragons, who carry the Divine Feminine energies of the Moon and the pure white dragons from Lyra, who offer the codes of the unicorn kingdom. They are clearance experts and can transmute lower energies and illuminate higher ones.

Here is an invocation that you might like to use to connect with them:

> *I now invoke a silver lunar dragon and a dragon from Lyra to clear any dense energy in my causal chakra.*
>
> *I invoke my beloved unicorn to purify and illuminate the chamber as it opens.*
>
> *I invoke Archangel Christiel to help me integrate all that I need for peace.*
>
> *So be it.*

VISUALIZATION FOR ETERNAL PEACE

- Take a moment to relax and focus on your breathing.

- See or sense your causal chakra like a pure white moon above your head.

- Imagine you are waiting quietly inside it.

- Archangel Christiel enters and enfolds you in his white feathery wings.

- Relax into the peace and stillness.

- Feel your aura becoming a deep serene white.

- The pearl-studded gates open wide and you step into the angelic realms.

- Enjoy meeting angels and unicorns.

- Feel their love and their peace touching you.

Chapter 34

The Journey to Soul Wisdom

Your soul has been on a very long journey, through many dimensions, on various planets and in different universes, gathering gifts, talents, knowledge and wisdom. Every experience has been in order to understand love, and all are recorded in your Soul Star chakra.

The Soul Star chakra

This glorious magenta chakra with 33 chambers has two parts. Archangel Zadkiel is in charge of transmuting energy in the lower section, while Archangel Mariel overlights the higher chambers. In these, you access the true keys to mastery and move into a much higher vibration to start the journey to merge with your Monad. There are doorways to past-life gifts, knowledge and wisdom in this chakra, and all your wisdom from the Golden Era of Atlantis.

Planetary and cosmic Soul Star chakras

The Soul Star chakra of the planet is Agra in India, where Shah Jahan built the Taj Mahal as a memorial of his true love for his wife.

The cosmic Soul Star is Orion, the constellation of wisdom.

The journey through the Soul Star chakra

The experiences of the lower chambers of this chakra offer really important lessons in love. Being a parent takes you automatically through these. However, if you do not have children of your own, you can follow this path with someone else's child or animal, or you may have learned these lessons in a past life. Some people have these experiences through service, for example nursing the sick or undertaking charity work. These lower chambers may even be fully open before you incarnate for this life.

As you take the journey through the lower chambers, your unicorn, Archangel Zadkiel and a Gold and Silver Violet Flame dragon will be focusing their energy onto this chakra.

You may like to use this invocation to call them to you:

I now invoke a Gold and Silver Violet Flame dragon to clear any dense energy in my Soul Star chakra.

I invoke my beloved unicorn to purify and illuminate the chambers as they open.

I invoke Archangel Zadkiel to help me transmute all that is not higher love.

I ask Archangel Mariel for divine assistance to ascend through the Soul Star chakra.

So be it.

- **Chamber 1**: In the first chamber, the lesson is to love yourself. This is about accepting yourself as you are, unconditionally, without any judgement. If you think or say something self-deprecating, ask Archangel Zadkiel to transmute it and replace it with self-esteem.

- **Chamber 2**: See your parents as vulnerable humans who are or were doing their best with their conditioning and consciousness, and love them.

- **Chamber 3**: Recognize that animals are beautiful spirits in physical bodies, just as you are, and love them.

- **Chamber 4**: In this chamber, open your heart to loving your siblings, cousins or close family. Actively keep the connections open to them.

- **Chamber 5**: Love your teenage self. Few teenagers have an easy passage, so forgive yourself for anything that may have happened at this time in your life.

- **Chamber 6**: Help and serve others with love. If you do not do so already, the universe will present you with opportunities when you are ready for them.

- **Chamber 7**: Be content and happy with yourself as a male or female or other. Rejoice in who you are.

- **Chamber 8**: When you are in love, you see your own beautiful aspects reflected in the other. They make you feel lovable, beautiful and special. Consciously see those parts of yourself and love that you.

- **Chamber 9**: Experience the joy of making someone else happy.

- **Chamber 10**: Love your parents for all they have done to bring you to this stage. Acknowledge their good qualities and those that challenged you to grow.

- **Chamber 11**: Experience serving with love your own child or a soul you can have an influence on.

- **Chamber 12:** In this chamber, reach a new level of loving yourself.

- **Chamber 13:** Whether you are a mother or father or connected closely with a baby, this lesson is about loving that soul. You may immediately be filled with love because you are greeting an old friend. However, you may never have connected with the soul before, so are unfamiliar. You may even have had a difficult connection with them in another lifetime, and this may make it hard to love them. But you learn the lesson of this chamber when you open up to doing so.

- **Chamber 14:** The lesson here is about loving your partner deeply. You may have done so in another incarnation or you may have connected with a soul-mate with whom you had a pure love.

- **Chamber 15:** Not everyone takes immediately to parenthood, so in this chamber your test is to love learning to be a parent. If you have not had the opportunity in this life, you have almost certainly done so in others.

- **Chamber 16:** Here you must expand your higher heart and let the child love other people.

- **Chamber 17:** Appreciate the grandparents and recognize that they are or were beings of their time, with their own conditioning.

- **Chamber 18:** Spread your love outside your family, especially if you are a tight unit.

- **Chamber 19:** Learn to nurture yourself, for you cannot truly nurture another until you can cherish yourself.

- **Chamber 20:** We are all one, and within that oneness there is variety. In this chamber, you love and appreciate the difference between your child and other people's children.

- **Chamber 21**: The soul in your charge is precious and here you are able to trust them with others.

- **Chamber 22**: And the lesson here is slightly different, as you trust others with your child.

- **Chamber 23**: When you and your partner have a baby, you become a unit of three and your relationship with your community changes. In this chamber, you re-establish yourself in the community.

- **Chamber 24**: Here you practise working in harmony with your partner.

- **Chamber 25**: You care for your parents.

- **Chamber 26**: The greatest gift you can give your family, especially your child, is to be happy. Then they can relax and feel free to be happy too.

- **Chamber 27**: As your child grows, you have to learn to let go of the reins and allow them to be more independent.

- **Chamber 28**: Here you must accept yourself as you grow older.

- **Chamber 29**: Love who you are.

- **Chamber 30**: Love other people as they are.

- **Chamber 31**: When your child moves towards adulthood, you must set them free so that they can be independent and live their own life.

- **Chamber 32**: As your parents grow old, you have to set them free to live the old age they want or to pass over.

- **Chamber 33:** The final chamber is about your spiritual growth and preparing yourself to ascend to the highest part of the Soul Star chakra.

Archangel Mariel in his glorious magenta light overlights you now.

VISUALIZATION TO EXPLORE YOUR SOUL JOURNEY

- A golden staircase leads to a massive diamond-studded doorway. This opens into a beautiful and wondrous temple.

- Archangel Mariel stands in the centre of the temple, holding a golden key.

- He hands you the key and you accept it.

- It opens a golden door, beyond which are held the gifts, knowledge and wisdom acquired during your long soul journey.

- You may take as long as you like to explore them.

- Then steps to your Stellar Gateway appear and you start to climb to another glorious level.

Chapter 35

In Tune with the Infinite

A vast pure gold chalice above your head, beyond your outstretched arms, is your Stellar Gateway, the chakra that is in the charge of Archangel Metatron and the wondrous Seraphim Seraphina.

The Stellar Gateway

The Stellar Gateway has 12 chambers or petals, each of which holds an ascension quality: wisdom, integrity, strength, courage, vision, peace, compassion, balance, oneness, truth, love and joy. When you have totally mastered all of these qualities, you can merge with your Monad, your original divine spark, the true essence of who you are, which contains the sum total of all your experiences. This is the ultimate ascension. It is seventh-dimensional ascension. This is the level that the Illumined Masters achieved on Earth.

Planetary and cosmic Stellar Gateway chakras

The Stellar Gateway of the planet is the Arctic, an area that has been purified with ice so that it can hold the high-frequency energy necessary for this chakra.

The Stellar Gateway of the cosmos is the planet Mars, the ascended aspect of which is called Nigellay. Mars is third-dimensional and reflects the martial energy we have seen for aeons on Earth. The part that has ascended holds the frequency of the spiritual leader and peacemaker, with the authority, power and wisdom to hold the entire universe together in peace and contentment. As the universe becomes fifth-dimensional, Mars/Nigellay will come into its true power and glory.

Archangel Metatron

The golden orange Archangel Metatron is in charge of the ascension of many individuals, the planet and the universe! His Metatron Cube holds all the sacred geometry for ascension.

Seraphim Seraphina

There are 144 12th-dimensional Seraphim who chant the sounds of creation round the Godhead. They do not usually work with humanity, and we are blessed that Seraphina does, mainly as head of the intergalactic training schools.

The paths to higher ascension

When you reach the Antakarana bridge from your Soul Star to your Monad and then to Source, you are offered a choice. You can walk towards higher ascension on one or more of several paths. Many current aspirants are choosing to take all the paths together. All of them will eventually enable you to merge with your I AM Presence. None is better than any other; they are just different.

The sapphire path

When you walk the sapphire path, you work with Archangel Michael. You focus on communication with integrity, higher knowledge and taking action. Archangel Michael offers you his protection and strength and expects you to act with honour, truth and trust.

The emerald path

When you walk the emerald path, you work with Archangel Raphael, who lights your way. This is the path of healing, abundance consciousness, knowledge, wisdom and ultimately enlightenment. Archangel Raphael helps you to see everything from a higher perspective.

The ruby path

Archangel Uriel, the Angel of Peace and Wisdom, guides you on the ruby path. He helps you develop confidence and self-worth and expects you to act and communicate wisely and to spread peace. If you are ready, he encourages you to take intergalactic responsibility.

The rainbow path

The Seraphim Seraphina guides and helps you on the rainbow path, where you attend her intergalactic training schools on the inner planes. There is more about this path in the next chapter.

The diamond path

This is the path of purity, clarity and joy. Archangel Gabriel influences you to find the spiritual discipline to attain this pure state and inspire others to walk with you.

The golden path

This is the angelic path. Here, you work with the angelic realms and radiate a golden energy as you stay attuned to them and develop angelic qualities.

The Antakarana bridge

When your Soul Star chakra is fully open and active, a rainbow bridge starts to form from it to your Stellar Gateway, your I AM.

As you construct this Antakarana bridge with love, higher thoughts and spiritual practice, your Monad starts to build the bridge down to meet you.

Here is an illustration of what happens. Your Monad, soul and personality on Earth are like one huge family. Your Monad represents your grandparents. When they grow up, their children travel to all parts of the world to learn about different countries and experience them. At first they communicate, but gradually the connection gets more tenuous, though it is never fully lost. And then the grandchildren in their turn go off to explore the planet. The grandparents hope that one day their children and grandchildren will return and tell them all about their adventures and what they have learned. First the grandchildren go home to their parents. This happens metaphorically when your Soul Star chakra opens and you are in touch with all your soul energies. And then you are ready to step onto the Antakarana path back to your grandparents' home. As soon as they know you are on your way, they set off down the path to meet you. There is a huge celebration when the family meets again.

Whichever path you take, or if you embrace all the paths together, it is important to make sure your 12 chakras are open and spinning before you do the spiritual or service work to build your Antakarana bridge to your Monad. Below is an easy exercise to prepare your chakras.

VISUALIZATION THROUGH THE CHAKRAS

Preparing to step onto the Antakarana bridge

- Find a place where you can be quiet and undisturbed, perhaps in your sacred space or by your altar. However, you can also practise this while walking in a forest or by a river or ocean or anywhere in nature.

- Focus on your Earth Star chakra and see or sense it spinning and radiating bright sparkling silver light.

- See or sense your base chakra spinning and radiating shimmering platinum light.

- See or sense your sacral chakra spinning and radiating glorious transcendent pink light.

- See or sense your navel chakra spinning and radiating bright luminous orange light.

- See or sense your solar plexus chakra spinning and radiating bright golden wisdom.

- See or sense your heart chakra spinning and radiating pink-white rays of love.

- See or sense your throat chakra spinning and radiating a powerful royal blue.

- See or sense your third eye chakra spinning and radiating a shimmering crystal green.

- See or sense your crown chakra spinning and radiating crystal yellow.

- See or sense your causal chakra spinning and radiating soft moonlight white.

- See or sense your Soul Star chakra spinning and radiating glorious magenta.

- Way above you, see or sense your Stellar Gateway, a wondrous golden orange chalice, opening wider and wider.

- See or sense your chakra column becoming a unified field of light.

- Be aware of Archangel Metatron on your right-hand side, holding the Divine Masculine for you.

- Archangel Sandalphon is on your left-hand side, holding the Divine Feminine for you.

- They stand like sentinels reaching from the centre of Earth to the heavens.

- You are in divine balance.

- From your Soul Star chakra, a rainbow bridge of light streams out as far as your eyes can see. It is your Antakarana bridge.

- Dragons are spiralling round it, protecting it.

- Relax and breathe comfortably, knowing that as you open yourself up to your Antakarana bridge, it is automatically being built. You are starting to make a connection to your Monad.

Stepping onto your Antakarana bridge

- First humbly ask how you can best serve.

- There is a moment of silence in the universe as Archangels Sandalphon and Metatron bless you.

- From now on, every thought you think and every word you say must be directed towards your I AM.

- You are moving through new wavelengths and dimensions into a much higher frequency.

- You are in tune with the Infinite.

Part IV

Higher Ascension Tools to Propel You into the Golden Future

Chapter 36

Healing Old Programming

The techniques in this part of this book are incredibly powerful and will raise you to the upper levels of the fifth dimension or even into the sixth dimension for a short time. The higher your frequency, the more you attract good things into your life, enhance your personal ascension journey and help to bring forward the energies of the golden future.

The first step is to heal old programming. Every single person or situation is in your life because you have drawn it in with your unconscious programming. During your soul journey you have absorbed thousands and thousands of beliefs and programmes, all of which accumulate to create your current circumstances, your health, your body.

The beliefs you have programmed in
your consciousness create your life.

If you aren't happy with your life, remember your essence is divine. Your Higher Self is love and your Monad, the divine within you, is 12th-dimensional light. Your beliefs are the only things that stop you from living a glorious, abundant, healthy and love-filled life.

How can you create a better life?

Gratitude

Gratitude is a magnetic energy that attracts good things. In our day-to-day lives we have hundreds of opportunities to be grateful. However, it is very easy to say 'please' and 'thank you' in a totally mechanical and meaningless way.

I remember saying to my children when they asked for something, 'And what's the magic word?' They would trot out, 'Please,' or, 'Thank you,' automatically. It worked as a limited key to receiving what they wanted; it did not unlock my heart. But whenever one of them open-heartedly asked or thanked me for something, my heart would open in response and I would move mountains to give them what they wanted.

In many cases, 'thank you' has become a ritual. Someone opens a door for you and you respond with an automatic 'Thanks.' It is just a word and you have forgotten it in a moment and so have they. It has no energetic impact. However, when you say a heartfelt 'Thanks,' an energetic exchange takes place and a flame lights in both your hearts. It leaves a pinprick of light in your soul.

This is even more so when you are grateful to your Monad or the universe. Your Monad is like a personal sun bringing you divine joy, warmth and nourishment that you often take for granted. When you are grateful instead, that pinprick of light in your soul can become millions of pinpricks, which form a huge flame of gratitude. This is seen by your Monad, who takes a step closer to you.

When you are truly grateful, the donor
automatically wants to give you more. When
you give thanks to the universe or your Monad,
they too want to heap abundance on you.

We can give thanks to our Monad for overlighting our lives, for the energy it is passing through us every day, for the divine light in our cells, for the joy and opportunities it brings us.

Here is a suggested gratitude prayer. Yours may be different, so do please change it to suit yourself.

Beloved Monad,

I offer heartfelt thanks for the light you shine through me every day, for the way you keep my body working and feed my cells with divine nourishment, for all you help me see with enlightened eyes.

Thank you for teaching me through the animal, bird and nature kingdoms.

Thank you for your constant unwavering presence.

I accept your gifts and healing with joy.

Apology

'Sorry' is another word that can be ritualistic or heartfelt. I recall my daughter telling me about a child who had come to tea. As they had stood on the doorstep saying goodbye, the mother had said to the little girl, 'Now, what do you say?' The child had looked totally confused for a moment, then replied hopefully, 'Sorry!'

There is a huge difference between a casually grunted, automatic, 'Sorry,' when you bump into someone and a heartfelt, 'I'm so sorry.' Much litigation would be unnecessary if people offered a genuine apology.

Anything said from the heart dissolves barriers and brings people's defences down.

Saying 'sorry' and genuinely meaning it also dissolves stuck energies that may have accumulated through your soul's journey.

Saying a genuine open-hearted 'sorry' to your Monad for all the lower choices you have ever made enables your divine self to embrace you.

Ho'oponopono

Hermes, one of the High Priests of Atlantis, took his tribe to Hawaii after the fall, where they became the kahunas.

One of the powerful healing prayers they brought with them was the *Ho'oponopono* prayer:

I am sorry. Please forgive me. Thank you. I love you.

Its simplicity is its power. You apologize, ask for forgiveness, express gratitude and then express love.

It works on two principles:

- You understand that we are all one.

- You accept that you are totally responsible for everything that is in your life.

It is your Monad that you are addressing with this prayer:

- You are talking to the divine you, and the divine can transmute old programmes.

- You are apologizing to your Monad for still holding the beliefs that block your progress.

- You are asking it for forgiveness. In your plea for forgiveness, you are asking the divine to dissolve the block.

- You are thanking your Monad for transmuting as much of that programming as possible.

- Then you are sending love to your Monad.

If you have a whole cluster of beliefs round a theme, you may need to say this many times.

Here are some examples.

A relationship

A friend moans about her child, partner or colleague. That friend is part of you, for you are one. You may recognize that you, too, sometimes feel frustrated with your child, partner or colleague. What belief causes this? It may be a belief about not being acknowledged, or appreciated, or loved or something else. Or you may not understand why you feel frustrated.

Say to your Monad:

I am sorry [for holding on to the belief that has created this].

Please forgive me [and dissolve the block this has created].

Thank you [for transmuting this belief].

I love you [and I know this helps me to align with you].

Judgement

You are walking down the road. You see someone behaving in a certain way and a judgemental thought arises. But that person is part of you! You are judging your divine essence. And judgemental thoughts separate us from oneness.

Say to your Monad:

I am sorry [for holding on to this judgemental belief].

Please forgive me [and dissolve the block this has created].

Thank you [for transmuting this belief].

I love you [and I know this lights up my divine self].

Television and social media

These are brilliant for bringing up stuff within us all. You see something nasty and a fearful or angry thought arises. Emotion arises from a belief. What is it?

Say to your Monad:

I am sorry [for holding on to the belief that has created this feeling].

Please forgive me [and dissolve the block this has created].

Thank you [for transmuting this belief].

I love you [and wish to acknowledge this].

Self-criticism

Most of us have been raised to put ourselves down. But if you catch yourself thinking, *I'm so stupid*, or, *I'm fat*, or, *I'm bound to fail*, or, *I bet I catch a cold*, or a million other things, *stop!*

The Violet Flame is great for cancelling a statement. Use it by saying the words, 'Cancel, Violet Flame,' but then say to your Monad:

I am sorry [for clinging to this negative programming].

Please forgive me [and dissolve the block this has created].

Thank you [for dissolving and healing it].

I love you [and wish to acknowledge this].

Pain or illness

This mostly comes from personal or ancestral beliefs that hold back your ascension. It does not matter that you do not know what the beliefs are or where they come from. Say or think:

I am sorry, please forgive me. Thank you. I love you.

Saying something is one stage deeper than a thought. In the last few days I have heard people say these and many other separation statements aloud:

- 'I'll never belong, because I am a foreigner.'

- 'I hope she doesn't come to this meeting.'

- 'I wish they'd go away.'

- 'All politicians are corrupt.'

Because we are one, the fact that I've heard them means that these sentiments are lost somewhere deep in my consciousness, so I've been saying the *Ho'oponopono*.

The power of the Ho'oponopono transmutes
your undesired programming so that you
return to oneness and mastery.

VISUALIZATION TO CHANGE
YOUR OLD PROGRAMMING

- Find a place where you can be quiet and undisturbed.

- Close your eyes and breathe comfortably.

- Mentally tell the universe that you are now ready to dissolve old outdated programming.

- Ask to receive higher light codes that replace the old with new life-affirming ones.

- Ask Archangel Metatron to place you in his golden orange ninth-dimensional ascension bubble of light.

- Take time to absorb the energy.

- Ask Archangel Gabriel to place his shimmering white cosmic diamond filled with joy and divine love over you.

- Sense it transmuting the old and filling you with new higher frequencies.

- Call in the seventh-dimensional Gold Ray of Christ.

- Sense it dissolving old conditioning and surrounding you with golden white love full of codes of wisdom and love.

- Imagine you are at peace and send out harmless thoughts.

- A cloak of invisibility is placed over you. You are completely safe everywhere.

- When you have absorbed these higher light codes, open your eyes.

Chapter 37

Your Angelic Essence and How to Protect It

In this chapter I am sharing some techniques that will enable you to accelerate your frequency into higher ascension, and this will prepare you for the golden future.

Your angelic essence

When your original divine spark left Source, angelic energy was placed in your essence and this is within you still. This means you can merge with your seventh-dimensional angelic self when you are ready. Then, as you activate your seventh-dimensional aspect, you naturally attract wonderful things.

However, your bright light also draws in lower frequencies that want to steal or extinguish your energy, so you need special protection for your energy fields.

If you work with seventh-dimensional energies,
you need seventh-dimensional protection.

I suggest some forms of protection below. Different ones work for different people. Whatever you trust and believe in, based on the personal experiences you have had on your soul journey, will work for you. Take time to try out different ones and notice how they make you feel. You can also use them to protect the energy in your home or workplace.

Seventh-dimensional protection

Red and gold light from Hollow Earth

Hollow Earth is seventh-dimensional and here you can access a magnificent protective red and gold light of energy and wisdom.

- Draw the red and gold energy up from Hollow Earth.

- Allow this to spread over your aura so that it adds a seventh-dimensional layer of protection and wisdom around your fields. This will enable you to ground the seventh-dimensional energy coming in from the universe. It will protect you totally from any lower vibrations.

- You can also visualize this red and gold light from Hollow Earth round our planet to protect it. You can even send it out into the universe.

When you can truly cope with this high-frequency energy, the red will change to blue. At that point, the blue will draw in the pain of the world and heal it. If you carry this blue in your aura, you will be one of the world's healers.

Archangel Metatron's protection

As we approach the golden future, there are many new high-frequency energies coming in. These incredible light energies will feel very different from those to which you have become accustomed. Therefore you will need special protection until you are used to them.

You can call in Archangel Metatron's golden orange ninth-dimensional ascension bubble of light. This helps you to absorb the energy with its higher light codes. It will also protect you from the third-dimensional vibrations currently on Earth.

To access this, just ask Archangel Metatron to place his golden orange bubble around you and your energy field.

Archangel Gabriel's cosmic diamond

Archangel Gabriel's diamond works on many frequency levels.

If you invoke his seventh-dimensional cosmic diamond and really feel it surrounding your energy fields, you will have powerful protection. It will also raise your vibration.

The cosmic diamond causes lower beings or energies to bounce off it and nothing can penetrate its purity. When it surrounds you, it purifies your aura and transmutes any stuck energy that is ready to be released. The facets within the diamond light up and enhance your own special gifts. The cosmic diamond does considerably more than protect you and transmute lower energies, though, for it also ignites joy and divine love within you.

The seventh-dimensional Gold Ray of Christ

If you have worked with Jesus or with Christ energy in past lives or this one, this golden white protection will be particularly effective.

Simply invoke the seventh-dimensional Gold Ray of Christ and allow it to form a golden white ball of light right round you. The wisdom and love within it dissolve lower energies and form a protective shield around you.

The ball of harmlessness

The greatest protection of all is harmlessness. When you are truly harmless, you are totally safe. No person or animal feels threatened, so they relax their defences and walk on by! No insect will sting you, nor barb or prickle touch you. A warrior draws attack, but if you are totally harmless, you can walk through a battlefield. This is very advanced protection. To use it, watch your thoughts and attitudes. The more harmless your thoughts and emotions, the safer you will be.

Harmlessness confers invisibility, too. To wear a cloak of invisibility, you must be harmless and totally in tune with your surroundings.

VISUALIZATION TO PROTECT
YOUR ANGELIC ESSENCE

- Find a place where you can be quiet and undisturbed.

- Take a moment to breathe deeply and relax.

- Focus deep in your heart and visualize your golden core of angelic light.

- Call in red and gold light from Hollow Earth.

- Watch the magnificent energy rise up and surround your aura.

- Call in Archangel Metatron's golden orange ninth-dimensional ascension bubble.

- See or sense this forming another layer of protection around you.

- Call in the cosmic diamond to surround your expanded aura in its glittering light.

- Sense it transmuting lower energies, then feel your heart being touched by joy and divine love.

- Call in a seventh-dimensional golden white ball of Christ Light.

- A vast ball of pure love and protection settles over the other forms of protection.

- And now focus on your angelic centre of angelic light, peace and harmlessness.

- Affirm that your thoughts, words and actions are totally harmless to all creatures.

- Know that to the extent this is true, you are protected by a cloak of invisibility.

- Sit quietly, sensing which forms of protection are most effective for you.

Chapter 38

Your Mighty I AM

In preparation for the new Golden Age, huge waves of light and energy are coming into the planet. This is waking more people up and taking many to a much higher frequency than has been available since the Golden Era of Atlantis.

You have been taking instructions from your soul. Now it is time to connect with the glorious ineffable light of your Monad or I AM, your original divine spark from Source, the great blazing flame that is your true essence.

Your divine master blueprint

Your I AM is your divine master blueprint. It is your divine plan, your fixed design.

Here is an analogy. Imagine that you, that is your personality self, have built a small house on a plot of land, and gradually, as you have evolved towards your soul, you have extended and expanded it. But the architect's original plan, that is your Monad's design or vision, was for a large and magnificent mansion, radiant with light and full of everything your heart desired. This original blueprint has always been there waiting, but now you are ready for it! Yes, now!

Archangel Metatron is preparing you to accept your divine master blueprint now.

When you accept this, your life transforms. You are your own authority. You know exactly what your life purpose is. With every breath and thought, you are carving out the life you choose.

I AM the Monad

Here is a powerful way of accessing the light of your essence, your wondrous, magnificent self. It came from Djwhal Khul through Alice Bailey. You may well know it already.

Close your eyes and say:

I AM the Monad.

I AM the light divine.

I AM love.

I AM will.

I AM fixed design.

I AM affirmations or decrees are immensely powerful. They come from the part of you that is pure brilliant dazzling white light – the angelic part of you, your original divine spark.

Here is an explanation of the above decree:

- 'I AM the Monad' is another way of saying, 'God and I are one,' or, 'I AM that I AM.' It affirms that you merge totally with your Monad. You accept your wondrous spiritual heritage.

- 'I AM the light divine' literally affirms that you align with your divine light. This is not a 60-watt bulb. Your divine light is of a frequency beyond the atom. It is your electronic self, your essence, at which point you are spiritual matter.

- 'I AM love.' Source love is held within the light of your true spiritual essence.

- 'I AM will' means that you surrender your free will and merge with the will of God.

- 'I AM fixed design' affirms that you now fully accept and live with the divine blueprint given to you by Source when your original spark or Monad was created. Until now, your Monad has appeared to be outside you, at a distance, up a ladder and out of reach. At last you are ready to connect with your true core. Within you is a fount of knowledge, wisdom and love, and the more you communicate with your divine essence, the more quickly you will notice the outcome in your life.

I AM white light

Some of you may know that over 20 years ago I founded the Diana Cooper School as a not-for-profit organization to train spiritual teachers all over the world.

One day while I was meditating, I unexpectedly found myself propelled to the retreat of the Great White Brotherhood. Here the Great Ones told me that our school was part of the White Brotherhood. Cathars, Essenes, Rosicrucians, Knights Templar, Druids and other sacred organizations all belong to the White Brotherhood. Soon after this meditation, and such a fabulous confirmation, we changed our name to the Diana Cooper School of White Light to acknowledge this special connection.

I started to say the following decree twice a day and I literally felt the white light in my aura intensify and my frequency rise very quickly:

Beloved I AM Presence,

Blaze your pure white light through me.

Transmute all lower frequencies

with their cause and effect,

past, present and future,

and replace them with divine love,

soul satisfaction and fulfilment.

So be it.

I find it is most powerful when I stand and visualize brilliant dazzling white light pouring down through me as I say this. I keep the white light flowing for a minute and often see protective golden Christ Light around it. Then I can radiate the energy out.

You can use this for yourself or adapt it to include members of your family, group or organization. We adapted it for the Diana Cooper School to embrace all the teachers. It helps to keep us all together within the blazing white flame and enables us all to radiate high-frequency energy into the world. The more white light there is in the world, the better!

The purer and more dazzling your white light, the greater your creative power. When held in pure brilliant dazzling white divine light, creative power is unwavering certainty. When you are relaxed and centred in the light, your thoughts manifest immediately. So, when you ascend to live within your I AM, it is your responsibility to control and direct your thoughts. You must also create with integrity from your blazing higher-dimensional heart.

The great Illumined Masters, who live fully within their divine electronic bodies, are of the finest ethereal matter. They radiate rays of light. They accept their divine right to have health, wealth, love, success and an abundance of their heart's desire. Naturally by the time they reach this level, their wish is always the will of God. There is no separation. They automatically create divine possibilities with their thoughts, as you do when you merge with your angelic self.

I am sharing three more particularly powerful I AM decrees that can accelerate your higher ascension. When you make an I AM decree with a person, your Monad merges with the light of that being and divine alchemy occurs. I will explain the energy each line calls in.

I AM Lady Venus

This I AM decree merges your Monad totally with Lady Venus, the High Priestess of Atlantis who became a goddess of love. Because she incarnated on Earth, she has a very good understanding of human love as well as love of humanity as a whole and cosmic love.

I AM Lady Venus.

I AM a goddess of love.

I AM the hand of friendship.

I AM the whisper of compassion.

I AM the touch of healing.

I AM the key to unity.

Let me explain what this really means.

- 'I AM Lady Venus' is the call to your Monad to meld its light with that of Lady Venus.

- 'I AM a goddess of love' specifically calls on your Monad to merge with the highest goddess aspect of unconditional love.

- 'I AM the hand of friendship.' Your hand is the extension of your heart centre that reaches out to help others. When you decree, 'I AM the hand of friendship,' it attunes you to the truest energy of neighbourliness and fifth-dimensional community.

- 'I AM the whisper of compassion' is your affirmation that your heart is now on a wavelength that responds to the call of humanity without becoming personally engaged.

- 'I AM the touch of healing.' This attunes you to the healing heart of Lady Venus and through her to the Cosmic Heart. It invites divine love and healing to flow into you and to touch others through you.

- 'I AM the key to unity.' With this statement you align yourself with those who hold this planet in oneness.

Whenever I say this, I can feel it vibrate through me, and I hope it touches you too!

I AM Lord Kumeka

Lord Kumeka is my guide and also my twin flame. He has never incarnated, so we are not destined to meet in the flesh. He stepped down from another universe to oversee the setting up of the Golden Era of Atlantis with Archangel Metatron. Now he has returned to serve our planet as the Master of the Eighth Ray, bringing transmutation, purification and enlightenment to humanity. He works on the wondrous clear Topaz Blue Ray.

If you resonate with Lord Kumeka, here is an I AM decree for you:

I AM Kumeka, Lord of Light.

I AM the Topaz Ray so bright.

I AM serene content.

I AM enlightenment.

I AM my inner Sun.

I AM all and we are one.

Here is an explanation:

- 'I AM Kumeka, Lord of Light' affirms that your Monad now fuses with Kumeka and his amazing qualities.

- 'I AM the Topaz Ray so bright.' This confirms the Topaz Blue Ray of Clarity and Enlightenment is merging with your very cells.

- 'I AM serene content.' Only when you are totally purified can you experience divine serenity and contentment. Serene content is an incredible divine state.

- 'I AM enlightenment.' You now see everything from a divine perspective.

- 'I AM my inner Sun.' Your inner Sun is your Divine Masculine light, which brings deep inner happiness and the ability to activate your potential.

- 'I AM all and we are one.' This is a decree of oneness, the highest expression of divinity.

I AM Lord Voosloo

Lord Voosloo was the highest-frequency High Priest to incarnate in Atlantis. He incarnated with the keys and codes to facilitate the jump-shift of that society into the extraordinary Golden Era. Aeons before that, he enabled the beings of Mu, the civilization before Lemuria, to jump-shift into a Golden Age.

He has returned to this universe as Master of the Ninth Ray to help us with our double-dimensional leap into the next Golden Age. His light is a beautiful crystalline yellow. When you merge with his energy, he helps you with your personal jump-shift into ascension.

I AM Lord Voosloo.

I AM the Sun beyond the Sun.

I AM the bringer of light.

I AM the master of harmony.

I AM the jump-shift in consciousness.

I AM the new Golden Age.

This is the explanation:

- 'I AM Lord Voosloo' calls on your Monad to blend fully with Voosloo's illumined light.

- 'I AM the Sun beyond the Sun.' This affirmation aligns you through the Sun with Helios, where the light containing the higher information and knowledge for this universe is created. It activates the Divine Masculine energy of the universe, which is the protective, active energy that makes things happen.

- 'I AM the bringer of light' allows you to connect with the light created in Helios and bring it through your energy systems.

- 'I AM the master of harmony' aligns the cells of your body with the harmonics of the universe.

- 'I AM the jump-shift in consciousness.' You are now commanding that the keys and codes that will take you to higher ascension be ignited within you.

- 'I AM the new Golden Age.' You align yourself totally with the blueprint of the new Golden Age.

Unicorns

Millions of unicorns, known as 'the purest of the pure', are returning to Earth now to help us ascend into the golden future. Here is an I AM decree to help you align with their pure and wondrous light:

I AM unicorn diamond white.

I AM the truest inner sight.

I AM the purest of the pure.

I AM transcendent love so sure.

I AM enlightenment.

I AM Heaven sent.

The meaning is as follows:

- 'I AM unicorn diamond white' affirms that diamond-white unicorn light is within your Monad and you are activating it with your decree.

- 'I AM the truest inner sight' increases your quiet and firm faith that you see the divine within all.

- 'I AM the purest of the pure' aligns your energy with the unicorn kingdom.

- 'I AM transcendent love so sure' calls the transcendent love within your I AM to pour into your soul.

- 'I AM enlightenment' affirms that you now see everything from a divine perspective.

- 'I AM Heaven sent' accepts that you have a task to do on Earth and are guided to accomplish it with the help of the unicorns.

VISUALIZATION TO MOVE
TOWARDS YOUR MONAD

- Sit comfortably in a quiet, safe place.

- See yourself setting off from your house up a mountain.

- You are walking towards a magnificent mansion at the top.

- It is blazing with light and this encourages you to keep moving towards it.

- At last you reach the door and knock for entry.

- A being radiating pure white light opens the door.

- You are enfolded in love and peace.

- You are allowed entry for a moment, so you step into the great hall.

- You are held in pure, brilliant, dazzling white divine light.

- And then you find yourself back where you started.

- Quietly chant, 'I AM that I AM.'

Chapter 39

The Pastel Rainbow Breath for Sixth- and Seventh- Dimensional Chakras

In this chapter I explain how Archangel Metatron communicated with me about repatterning our DNA by bringing light through the sacred geometry of the Metatron Cube. More on this in the following chapter. He asked me to start using the Pastel Rainbow Breath to prepare the physical body for this energetic shift.

The frequency that the Pastel Rainbow Breath is bringing through us is that of the sixth-dimensional chakras.

The sixth-dimensional chakras

The frequency has risen so much on the planet that we can now bring in the sixth-dimensional chakras, though not permanently. The exciting news is that when the sixth-dimensional chakra column has descended into our physical body, even if only for a moment, we can connect with our I AM Presence.

The colours of the sixth-dimensional chakras

The high-frequency colours of these chakras are pale, shimmering and translucent. The following are the colours I was given. They will change as humanity shifts. If you see or sense a different colour, follow your intuition and use what is right for you.

- **Stellar Gateway**: silver shimmering through ethereal golden orange

- **Soul Star**: silver shimmering through ethereal magenta

- **Causal**: silver shimmering through ethereal diamond white

- **Crown**: silver shimmering through ethereal crystal yellow

- **Third eye**: silver shimmering through ethereal crystal green

- **Throat**: silver shimmering through ethereal lilac

- **Heart**: silver shimmering through ethereal white

- **Solar plexus**: silver shimmering through ethereal gold

- **Navel**: silver shimmering through ethereal peach

- **Sacral**: silver shimmering through ethereal rose

- **Base**: silver shimmering through ethereal platinum

- **Earth Star**: pale translucent ethereal silver

The seventh-dimensional chakras

When you are ready to bring down the seventh-dimensional chakras, even if it is only for a fraction of a second, your connection with your Monad becomes much stronger.

The colours of the seventh-dimensional chakras

In these chakras, golden light is shimmering through the ethereal crystal colour:

- **Stellar Gateway**: gold shimmering through pale crystal golden orange

- **Soul Star**: gold shimmering through pale crystal magenta

- **Causal**: gold shimmering through pale crystal diamond white

- **Crown**: gold shimmering through pale crystal yellow

- **Third eye**: gold shimmering through pale crystal green

- **Throat**: gold shimmering through pale crystal lilac

- **Heart**: gold shimmering through pale crystal white

- **Solar plexus**: gold shimmering through pale crystal gold

- **Navel**: gold shimmering through pale crystal peach

- **Sacral**: gold shimmering through pale crystal rose

- **Base**: gold shimmering through pale crystal platinum

- **Earth Star**: gold shimmering through pale crystal silver

The Pastel Rainbow Breath

Archangel Metatron told me that this was one of the ways the people of the Golden Era of Atlantis were able to relax to a cellular level. The sixth or seventh-dimensional rainbow colours are such a high frequency that they can enter the cells and touch the electrons, which are the divine energies that fly above the nucleus within each atom, and the people of the Golden Era would breathe these rainbow colours into every part of their bodies.

Now, when you practise this, your sixth-dimensional chakra column can slip down into you.

Here is the breath I use. And again, if you sense or see different colours, use them, for that is right for you! If you want to do this exercise in a different way, follow your intuitive guidance.

Preparation

- Find a place where you can be comfortable and undisturbed.

- Prepare your space by lighting a candle, activating a crystal, spraying the room with high-frequency spray or in any other way you wish to.

- Sit or lie down, ground and protect yourself.

- Call in Archangel Metatron and the unicorns to overlight you.

The Pastel Rainbow Breath

- Breathe in comfortably.

- On consecutive out-breaths, send out the following colours (if you cannot see them, simply think them):

  Pale ethereal pink with silver light shimmering through it into the big toe of your right foot

  Pale ethereal yellow with silver light shimmering through it into the second toe of your right foot

  Pale ethereal peach with silver light shimmering through it into the third toe of your right foot

  Soft ethereal green with silver light shimmering through it into the fourth toe of your right foot

Pale ethereal blue with silver light shimmering through it into the little toe of your right foot

Soft ethereal silver through every part of your right foot

Pale ethereal gold with silver light shimmering through it through your right ankle

Pale ethereal lilac with silver light shimmering through it down your right leg

- Repeat with the left leg.

- Repeat with your right arm into the fingers and then with your left arm.

- Breathe the colours down your back, allowing your spine to surrender to them.

- Breathe the colours over or into your head and throat in a way that feels right for you.

- Breathe the colours over your body or into any organ in a way that feels right for you.

- Remind yourself that you are relaxing to a cellular level, so that the strands of your DNA can relax and reconnect.

When you feel you are ready, practise with the golden light of the seventh-dimensional chakras so that they may enter you for a moment. In the Golden Era of Atlantis, even the High Priests and Priestesses could only do this for a fraction of a second. But as we approach the new Golden Age, those who are ready can prepare to bring in the seventh-dimensional chakra column by using the Golden Rainbow Breath.

VISUALIZATION FOR RAINBOW LIGHT

- You can do this while taking a physical walk if you wish.

- Decide whether you wish to do this visualization with your sixth or seventh-dimensional chakra colours. You may need to write them down for reference.

- Visualize the sixth or seventh-dimensional chakra colours one at a time streaming over you.

- You now have a sixth or seventh-dimensional rainbow flowing around you.

- Imagine you are walking out in nature.

- Your rainbow aura is interacting with trees and flowers, animals and insects.

- Notice what happens and how this feels.

- Now you are walking through a town.

- Your rainbow aura is interacting with people.

- Notice what happens and how this feels.

Chapter 40

The Metatron Cube

O ne day as I sat half asleep on the sofa with the sun pouring down onto me, Archangel Metatron held a Metatron Cube in my aura and started to turn it. He shone light through it. For several days after that I would wake to find the Cube turning around me. It felt quite amazing and I knew important work was being done on me!

Metatron Cube

The Metatron Cube is a geometric tool that contains all the sacred geometry of this universe. It consists of 12 circles round a central one, and every point is linked.

The Metatron Cube works on many levels. On one level it represents Source, surrounded by their 12 universes. On another it shows the connectedness of our chakras with our Higher Self. On yet another, the universal Metatron Cube, it shows the connection of our chakras with the four ascension planets and constellations, Orion, Sirius, the Pleiades and Neptune. Whenever you look at it, something comes into alignment for you.

Archangel Metatron has indicated that when the Metatron Cube is placed above your head, he can pour his light through it to activate

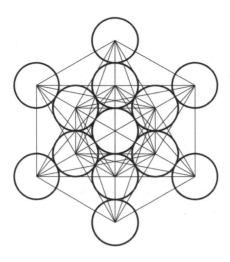

the geometry you need to start repatterning your DNA for the new Golden Age. When you bring in your sixth-dimensional chakras, he can hold the powerful geometric symbol over each one in order to overlay them with your personal sacred geometric patterning. Angels, dragons and unicorns will assist with this.

When the Metatron Cube is turned anti-clockwise, it pulls old stuck energy out of the chambers within your chakras, and when it is turned clockwise, high-frequency light is poured into the chakras through it.

DNA and why this is important now

Every cell of your body has a nucleus in its core. Within it is DNA, shaped like a double helix or two strands of beads slightly twisted. There are 64 codons or beads in each double helix and these give instructions for the functioning of your body. They also contain the codes for your hair, skin and eye colour, as well as inherited diseases or predispositions to certain illnesses. Every individual cell in your body contains the genetic code for your whole body.

The codes are based on spiritual
decisions taken before birth.

A predisposition is chosen by the soul, but there is not an inevitable outcome. Your thoughts and emotions, the food you eat, the way you live your life and your beliefs all impact greatly on your DNA.

When you are angry, hurt or stressed, or indulging in lower emotions, the strands tighten up so that the beads no longer connect with each other. Then you are like a TV that is not properly tuned in. So, when you are tense, you cannot tune in clearly to the messages from your soul or Monad.

At the fall of Atlantis, 44 out of 64 codes disconnected. Forty-four is the vibration of the Golden Era of Atlantis and represents the psychic and spiritual abilities that were taken away from us.

In order for your 12 strands of DNA to be reconnected and switched on again, you need to relax deeply and raise your frequency with love. When you are relaxed and contented, the codons touch each other and this means you are attuned to your divine potential and guidance from the highest. You can access your soul gifts. This will all happen automatically. The time is now.

When you are acting from your Monad or I AM and have total control over your thought processes, you can command the divine intelligence within your cells. In tune with your angelic self, you have the power to make anything happen. You can work through your atomic body to your electronic divine body. This is what the great Illumined Masters do, and it is the source of their power.

Your Mother Father God within

I remember Kumeka saying to me many years ago that the being that people thought of as God was in fact their own Monad. He said that no one in a human body could have any idea or concept of the true Ineffable Illumined Source of Creation from which their Monad came, so they translated their I AM into an external Godhead. This is perfectly understandable. Because your Monad is 12th-dimensional and in perfect harmony with the Source of All That Is, it steps its light down to you, its beloved child, to offer you all that you are ready to receive.

Your I AM is the wise all-knowing and
totally loving mother father within you. It is
your source of power and wisdom. It is totally
balanced masculine and feminine energy.

Once you unite with the I AM within, you have a fount of perfect nurturing and guidance. There is no need to look externally for instruction and advice.

Earlier, I discussed the importance and the power of creating wise, all-powerful, all-knowing, totally loving, compassionate, supportive and cherishing inner parents. Don't limit them to your ideal of fifth-dimensional guides; rather, expand them into the most beautiful love and light you can imagine. But even this is not enough to truly understand how extraordinary and magnificent the Mother Father God within you is.

To connect with your divine angelic parents more, communicate with them. Ask them for guidance and lovingly listen to their advice. Talk to them. Share your problems and let them lift you above those worldly concerns. They hold the perfect outcome and will illuminate you with this so that you take perfect decisions. The more often you do this, the more quickly you will receive their response, until your decisions are all divinely perfect.

Not only do your divine inner parents know everything that is happening in your universe, they understand everything that is going on within your personality self. They are fully aware of the extent to which you have overcome your ego in order to connect with them. They see the fears that you have faced, the emotions you have mastered, the lower self you have conquered. They love you and are proud of you. They know what you can do to bring about the best outcome.

Be grateful for them at all times. Thank them constantly for who they are and all they offer you. Divine inner parents are in some ways like perfect human parents. When a child is happily, joyfully grateful for what they are given, the parents want to give more. It is a universal law that joy-filled gratitude draws in more and more blessings.

As the wondrous light of your I AM within you showers you with gifts, love and adore your divine inner parents and see their glory and magnificence. Their light shines more brightly through you as you do so. Place the desires of your heart and soul in the light, and manifestations will come to you more quickly.

Cherish your divine inner parents. They know your every thought!

Imagine them holding you so that their love radiates through and from you. All will be well.

The more you consciously connect with your Mother Father God within, your I AM, the angelic white light within you, the more often and more quickly it will respond to you. Place your trust consistently in the Monad within you, and your personality self will gradually merge into its light. You will be an ascended master of great wisdom, love and light while in a physical body.

VISUALIZATION TO CONNECT WITH YOUR ANGELIC MOTHER FATHER LIGHT WITHIN

- Find a place where you can be quiet and relaxed.

- Close your eyes and take calming breaths.

- Call your angelic Mother Father self. Picture this in any way that feels right for you. Your divine parents may appear as a pure white light, or as people in a golden aura or in some other way.

- Remember the last time you had a problem, emotional or mental or even physical.

- Explain the problem and the feeling to your angelic Mother Father Light.

- Feel yourself merging into their light and love.

- Relax and know you are being transported to a higher frequency, to a glorious enlightened space.

- Rest here, calm, centred and trusting, for as long as you need to.

- While in their glorious angelic monadic energy, you have changed, so your universe can respond differently.

- Thank your angelic Mother Father Light and open your eyes.

Chapter 41

The Rainbow Path and Intergalactic Mastery

In the Golden Era of Atlantis, the High Priests and Priestesses were able to access the stars and bring back extraordinary illumined knowledge and wisdom to help their people. This is one of the ways in which Atlantis became such an advanced civilization, where the citizens were in touch with their Higher Selves and often their Monads.

In this current time, in order for Earth to step into its ascended glory as we reach the new Golden Age, a significant number of aspirants must have walked the rainbow path through Seraphina's Intergalactic Schools. Only then can we once more access the wisdom of the stars. Beings from many star systems, planets and constellations are again waiting in keen anticipation for us to make the connections.

The rainbow path takes you to higher ascension via the wondrous Seraphim Seraphina's intergalactic training establishments, where you meet many beings of the universe and may serve as an intergalactic emissary.

The gate to the rainbow path opens when your 12 chakras are fully engaged and you are ready to navigate your Antakarana bridge. At this point you are firmly on the ascension ladder.

Seraphina and Archangel Metatron

Seraphina is one of the few Seraphim to interact with humans in a physical body. She carries pure Divine Feminine energy and is seen in rainbow raiment. Archangel Metatron carries pure Divine Masculine energy and is seen as glorious golden orange light.

Together they will help you build your Antakarana bridge to the Intergalactic Schools of learning.

The invitation to walk the path

Archangel Metatron and Seraphina invite you onto the rainbow path when they see in your energy fields the rainbow lights that signify that you are a being of the universe who has an understanding of the importance of stellar connections.

Here are some indications that you may be a being of the universe:

- Do you look at the stars and know that there is life out there?

- Are you interested in space stories?

- Do you respond to talk of intergalactic masters?

- Do you see spaceships or find them in your photographs?

- Have you dreamed of Commander Ashtar, the commander of the Intergalactic Fleet of starships that protect this universe?

- Do you sense that you come from a distant place?

If you are interested in the rainbow path – and reading about it indicates that you are – you have already trained in many of the Intergalactic Schools in this universe. Your spirit may be attending classes there in your sleep. The purpose of connecting to the rainbow path is to go on a conscious journey, for it is time for you to recognize who you are.

Commander Ashtar

Commander Ashtar is the seventh-dimensional commander of the Intergalactic Fleet. His spaceships patrol this universe and are strategically placed round Earth to watch over and protect us.

Commander Ashtar serves on the Intergalactic Council, where his role is to maintain balance and harmony in the universes. He usually presents himself to us as a tall man with blond hair and blue eyes, dressed in silver-blue.

He originates from Helios, the Great Central Sun beyond our Sun, which radiates the Divine Masculine energy that bathes us all on Earth. He is also an avatar on Venus, the Divine Feminine.

The Great Crystal of Golden Atlantis is currently at the bottom of the ocean in the centre of the Bermuda Triangle. In 2015 Archangel Metatron and Commander Ashtar commanded that the etheric crystal rise again and realign to the Great Central Sun. It is now pouring incredible light over the world. Everyone is being touched by it.

Machu Picchu, Peru, is one of only four two-way inter-dimensional portals on Earth. One of Commander Ashtar's roles is to look after it and keep it clear. His vast mothership enters Earth through here and it is the only portal on Earth that can cope with a lightcraft of that size.

Service work to build your Antakarana bridge

Once you are on the rainbow path, you have special work to do. Only humans can do this. You are the channel through which stellar wisdom can be downloaded to people on Earth, in the same way that you are the bridge that allows angels to help people and situations on the planet.

A flame that links you to the stars

There are only seven places on Earth that can energetically hold the light of Commander Ashtar's mothership. In these places you can connect with the wisdom of ancient cultures already held in the land and merge it with the wisdom of the stars to which that place is connected. This creates a mighty flame of energy that you can leave here.

Each time you do this, it builds your Antakarana bridge and propels you powerfully towards your Monad.

Visit the seven places on Earth that can accommodate the mothership

Lake Taupō, New Zealand

The first of the places where the energy is pure enough to accommodate this light craft is in Lake Taupō, New Zealand. Here the wisdom and knowledge originally brought by the High Priestess Hera from Atlantis is stored in the land and in a crystal skull. It is held by the Māori culture.

As you read this, imagine yourself holding Hera's crystal skull containing mystic information and advanced knowledge. This place is connected to the Milky Way and Commander Ashtar beams light from there to you. The light in the land merges with the light from the Milky Way and forms a huge green light over you.

As you move away, you leave this great cosmic flame connecting New Zealand with the Milky Way. You receive wisdom.

Avebury, UK

Avebury, in the west country of England, is part of a massive portal that embraces Glastonbury and Stonehenge. Each of these incredible illumined places is also a portal in its own right. This used to be the welcome portal for spaceships from all the universes. Beings from all the stars, planets and constellations would come here to enjoy the love that enfolded them. Ancient Druid wisdom is held in the land here, as well as the light of the Inter-universal White Brotherhood. The grand inclusive portal is connected directly to the Cosmic Heart, Venus.

Your task here is to absorb the light held in the land and merge it with that pouring down through from the Cosmic Heart. You will be sitting or standing in a vast white-pink sparkling flame.

When you have absorbed the love energy you need, leave the flame lighting up the entire area.

Uluru, Australia

Uluru is a glorious sacred space that holds Lemurian wisdom. The portal there is being prepared to accept more spacecraft, so that wise cosmic travellers can help the entire world. Lemurian energy is held by the Aboriginal peoples, the original ones who took physical bodies at the end of that Golden Age. They grounded the knowledge and maintained their civilization through their connection with the Sun, which provided masculine force to balance their feminine energy.

As you read this, connect to the Lemurian light in the land at Uluru and open up to receive a shaft of light from the Sun. Sense the huge golden flame that has formed over you. In a few moments, see the flame linking the centre of our planet and the Sun. Accept Lemurian wisdom.

Guatemala

The next portal big enough for Commander Ashtar's mothercraft is Guatemala in Central America. This is another welcome portal connected to Venus, and the people here already embrace the knowledge and wisdom of visitors from the universe.

Aphrodite, a High Priestess of Atlantis, originated from Venus. At the fall of Atlantis, she took her tribe to South America and they became the Mayans. Their advanced knowledge of astronomy, mathematics and stellar connections is held in the land. As you read these words, allow yourself to connect with it, then open to receive a download of pure love from the Cosmic Heart. You may sense the great flame of pure love and wisdom that surrounds you now.

Know that you are leaving this flame in Guatemala.

The Himalayas

The Himalayan mountains are very pure and ancient, a vast and perfect place to accommodate the mothership. The land is full of higher ancient wisdom, so allow yourself to accept what is right for you. Then receive a download of cosmic light from Orion, the constellation of wisdom. As you feel the pure white flame embracing you, you are asked to be a wise one.

Leave your flame of wisdom in the mountains of the Himalayas.

Mount Shasta, USA

The land around Mount Shasta in California has been purified by snow and by Archangel Gabriel's light. It is a vast and pure portal. The land is full of Lemurian wisdom and love of nature, so you may like to tune in to it as you read these words.

This portal is connected to the Pleiades, so feel the healing blue from that constellation merging with the Lemurian wisdom around you. Have a sense that you are standing in the centre of an enormous blue healing flame that extends between Heaven and Earth. Absorb the healing.

When you move on, be aware of the blue flame lighting up the world.

The Hollow Earth portal, USA

The huge Hollow Earth portal in the United States forms a circle over Oklahoma, Kansas, Nebraska, South Dakota and the bottom of North Dakota.

There is much ancient Native American spiritual energy held in the land here. Imhotep, a mighty High Priest of Atlantis, brought his tribe here. They became the Cherokees, wise ones who held the secrets of Atlantis and much shamanistic knowledge and formed the basis of the Native American culture.

Have a sense of the wisdom here that connects you right down into the pyramid of Hollow Earth and merge it with a flame of blue light from the Pleiades. Stand in the centre of an enormous blue and white flame, absorbing the energy, and leave it behind you to radiate light from this portal.

Machu Picchu, Peru

Machu Picchu in Peru is the only portal on Earth that can accommodate Commander Ashtar's vast mothercraft, so it must enter and exit Earth through here. Each time you connect with Commander Ashtar and travel on his mothership, you will pass through this portal and you will automatically receive downloads of light from the Incas, who were brought here by the High Priest Thoth at the end of Atlantis.

VISITING COMMANDER ASHTAR'S MOTHERSHIP

- Find a place where you can be quiet and undisturbed.

- Close your eyes and relax.

- In front of you appears a rainbow-coloured lift.

- Step inside it and think, *Commander Ashtar's mothership.*

- The lift ascends silently, taking you safely into new dimensions.

- When it stops, the doors open and a vast oval-shaped silver craft glides up to where you are standing. It is bigger than several ocean liners put together.

- It opens up, and as you step inside, you are enveloped in soft white light.

- The mighty Commander Ashtar, wearing a silver-blue spacesuit, welcomes you.

- As the door slides closed behind you, you look round and realize that it is using technology of our distant future.

- You see dozens of beings, of all shapes and sizes, from all over the universe. All are friendly and welcoming.

- Take the time to connect with some of them.

- Commander Ashtar himself leads you to a chamber, where you lie on a couch.

- He pours a silver-blue ray of light through you, aligning you with the energies you need for your soul journey.

Chapter 42

Triple Ascension Flames

Many masters and all the archangels can place over us their awesome Ascension Flames, containing the concentrated light of their creator and special keys to their qualities, which can ignite your own latent potential. When an Ascension Flame is placed over you, it will instantly raise your frequency and accelerate your ascension path.

The masters who hold the Ascension Flames have undergone many challenges and initiations in order to earn the right to do so. We all start with personal mastery, then progress through planetary and galactic to universal mastery. If you are reading this, you are on this path and may have achieved levels of mastery in other incarnations or on your soul journey.

Reading about the Ascension Flames will draw their energy to you and may affect you. If you close your eyes after you have read about them, then call them in and wait as they are placed over or around you, they will touch you at a profound level.

You can send them to other people and visualize them over them, but always do this under grace. This means that a person will only receive the energy if their Higher Self gives permission, so that it is right for them.

The power of three

I find that invoking an Ascension Flame is one of the quickest boosts to my light and energy. You can bathe in any of them individually. However, if you want a power burst and ascension acceleration, call in three! The power of three is very potent. I will explain how some of them work particularly well together.

Ascension Flames for purification

The Golden Christed Flame

The Golden Christed Flame is one of the most beautiful and powerful energies. It is held by Jesus, who is now the Bringer of Cosmic Love. The Golden Christed Flame raises your frequency and touches you with wisdom. The Christ Light within it protects your energy fields, heals you and bathes you in unconditional love. At the same time, it can purify you right down to a cellular level.

The Violet Flame

St Germain and Archangel Zadkiel hold the Violet Flame. This is an intensely powerful flame used for transmutation. Because its power was being misused, at the fall of Atlantis it was withdrawn and returned to the inner places. As the frequency of humanity started to rise, we earned the right to use it again, and at the Harmonic Convergence in 1987 it was brought back for everyone to use. If it is placed over your energy fields, it opens them up, so it should be used wisely with protection.

After a few years, the Gold and Silver Flames merged with it, so it became the Gold and Silver Violet Flame.

Later, Archangel Gabriel added his energy and it evolved into the Cosmic Diamond Violet Flame.

The latest upgrade is the Lilac Fire of Source.

You can use your intuition about which aspect is right for you to invoke at any given time.

The Pure White Flame of Atlantis

The wondrous Serapis Bey, who was a High Priest in the Golden Era of Atlantis, carries the pure white Ascension Flame of Atlantis. When you invoke it, it purifies you. It also holds keys and codes of Atlantis and can light up those within your energy fields that you are ready to bring forward.

This Flame also protects you from the effects of any lower energies you may be attracting, especially from Atlantean times. When you have received it, you may wish to concentrate it in the palms of your hands and then you can touch others with it.

VISUALIZATION TO BRING IN THE
TRIPLE PURIFICATION FLAMES

- First call in the Golden Christed Flame and let it come down through your body and fill your aura. This raises your frequency and protects your energy fields.

- Then you can safely bring the Violet Flame down into each of your chakras. When I invoke the three Flames together, I use the raw power of the Violet Flame alone. It helps to imagine or visualize violet flames flickering in each centre – Stellar Gateway, Soul Star, causal, crown, third eye, throat, heart, solar plexus, navel, sacral, base and Earth Star.

- Then, take a moment to prepare yourself before you invoke the Pure White Flame of Atlantis. Be aware of Serapis Bey holding this vast, extraordinary Flame and placing it slowly over the other two Flames that enfold you.

- Sit or stand in the three Flames and relax.

This potent combination is the ultimate in purification. Together, these three Ascension Flames can transmute any dark energies that are around you and also protect you from psychic attack. Never underestimate the power of these three Flames of purification.

Ascension Flames for personal unconditional love

Lady Nada, Pallas Athena and Lady Venus were all High Priestesses at the pinnacle of the Golden Era of Atlantis. Later they all became goddesses and Illumined Masters. Each one of them carries a different Ascension Flame of love that they can place into your heart or over you. These open you up to unconditional love so that you start to draw more true love into your life. As they expand, they also bathe you in cosmic love.

The Ascension Flame of Pure Love

Lady Nada is the twin flame of Sananda, the Higher Self of Jesus. She is the Lord of Karma for the Third Ray, spreading cosmic love round the universe, and Master of the Seventh Ray, the Ray of Ritual, Ceremony and Magic. *Nada* means 'nothing' and she is called Lady Nada because she has absolutely no ego. Her Ascension Flame is brilliant white-pink and it contains codes of ancient healing and wisdom as well as cosmic love.

The Ascension Flame of Love and Truth

Pallas Athena is known as the goddess of truth and she is the Lord of Karma for the Fourth Ray of Harmony and Balance. Her Ascension Flame shimmers blue-pink and holds codes of courage and wisdom. It helps you to cut through illusion with loving truth. When you bathe in this Flame, it ensures your heart is true, so that you attract honest relationships.

The Ascension Flame of Love and Harmony

Lady Venus is a goddess of love. Her Ascension Flame is glorious bright pink and carries the codes of purest love. It opens your heart to serene and beautiful loving relationships and connects you to the Cosmic Heart.

VISUALIZATION TO BRING IN THE TRIPLE FLAMES OF LOVE

- Open your heart centre and then invoke Lady Nada. Ask her to place her white-pink Flame of Pure Love right into your heart.

- See or sense the glorious Flame in your heart. Breathe into it and know it is healing you at a deep level and expanding your capacity to love with wisdom.

- And then be aware of Pallas Athena in front of you, holding up her shimmering blue-pink flame, which enables the frequency of your heart chakra to rise hugely. And open your heart wider.

- Finally Lady Venus, a goddess of love, looks into your eyes. She is holding the bright pink Ascension Flame of love with harmony. She places it in your heart and you breathe in.

- Take a moment to rest in the triple Flames of love. Then all three Flames reach out to touch the hearts of your family and friends and neighbours until you become a magnet for love.

- Now the Flames expand to surround our planet, then reach up to Venus, the Cosmic Heart. You receive a download of Source love. For an instant your loving essence encapsulates the world and everyone on it.

- Relax.

Every time you invoke these Flames, your loving core becomes stronger and brighter.

Ascension Flames for healing

The Flame of Divine Healing

This wondrous Healing Flame is carried by Jesus and is gold, pink and white, holding the purest energy of unconditional love. Love heals. This Flame is activated by your faith and is intensely powerful.

Mother Mary's Flame of Compassionate Healing

This Flame is Mother Mary blue with a golden centre. It is filled with qualities of love and compassion that open your heart to higher healing. It carries codes of kindness, gentleness and Divine Feminine wisdom, and fills you with qualities that allow you to feel whole.

Archangel Raphael's Healing Flame

Archangel Raphael's huge and magnificent emerald Healing Flame carries the keys and codes of your fifth-dimensional health blueprint. If you are ready, it will align your current health blueprint with that of your perfect divine possibility. Receive it with expectation and gratitude.

VISUALIZATION TO BRING IN THE
TRIPLE HEALING FLAMES

- Take a moment to open up to love and to affirm your faith before you invoke these Ascension Flames.

- The first is brought to you by Jesus, who is dressed in the purest white robes. He is holding His Flame aloft above your head with one hand, like a flaming gold, pink and white beacon. He touches your heart with his other hand before slowly bringing the Flame down. Sense it coming down over your head, shoulders, torso, hips and legs until it engulfs you, and give yourself time to breathe it in. Jesus stands on your right.

- Then Mother Mary steps towards you, holding in her hands the most delicate and beautiful blue Flame of Compassionate Healing. Before you prepare to bathe in it, look into her blue eyes, which are filled with understanding and healing. And then breathe in as she gently draws the Flame down over your body, then stands on your left.

- Archangel Raphael, the mighty Angel of Healing, places the emerald Healing Flame on the ground in front of you. As it flickers there, it becomes more transparent and you may even be able to sense or see your totally healthy divine self. Have a sense of your frequency rising to align with the energy of the Flame, then step into it and relax, allowing yourself to merge with your highest health possibilities. Archangel Raphael stands in front of you.

- See or sense Jesus, Mary and Archangel Raphael holding hands while you stand in the centre as the triple healing Flames work on you at a cellular level.

Chapter 43

Advanced Triple
Ascension Flames

In this chapter I introduce some even more powerful Ascension
Flame trios. Again, if you call them in and wait as they are placed
over or around you, they will touch you at a profound level.

Ascension Flames for peace

The Golden Flame of Peace with Wisdom

This Ascension Flame is held by Archangel Uriel. He is in charge
of your solar plexus chakra and this pure gold Flame helps to
enhance your self-worth and confidence. When you bathe in it, it
activates your power with wisdom, bringing forward your divine self
and your innate harmony.

The White Flame of Angelic Peace

Archangel Christiel holds the white Peace Flame. He is in charge
of your causal chakra, which is a peace chamber and entrance to
the angelic kingdom. Archangel Christiel also oversees the unicorn
kingdom. His Peace Flame brings you universal blessings, purity and

serenity. When it is placed over you, you may sense or see unicorns and Angels of Peace around you.

Buddha's Flame of Peace and Harmlessness

Lord Gautama was the first person from this planet to hold the position of the Buddha, the embodiment of wisdom. His Flame of Peace holds qualities of harmlessness, enlightenment and wisdom. It is citrine – a mixture of yellow wisdom and green harmony and balance.

VISUALIZATION TO BRING IN THE TRIPLE PEACE FLAMES

- Make sure you are in a harmonious space.

- First invoke the golden Flame of Peace with Wisdom and see Archangel Uriel holding aloft this flickering Flame before placing it slowly over you. Breathe comfortably as you feel its beautiful energy and allow it to work its magic.

- After this, call in the White Flame of Angelic Peace. You may sense or see Archangel Christiel bearing this Flame and you may be aware of tier upon tier of unicorns and Angels of Peace surrounding you as you open up to the flickering white fire. Know that you are receiving Codes of Peace.

- Finally, you may be aware of a vast translucent citrine Flame moving down towards you from the heavens. As it approaches and rests in front of you, let yourself feel total harmlessness and love for all, before you step into it and it lights you up.

- Take your time to breathe in every level of peace, serenity, tranquillity and harmlessness.

Ascension Flames for knowledge and wisdom

Lord Lanto, Lord Voosloo and Archangel Jophiel's Flames are all different hues of yellow, bringing in all the different qualities and kinds of knowledge and information as well as the wisdom to use them in the best possible way.

The other great master who works on a yellow ray is Lord Kuthumi, the World Teacher. He is currently bringing in a new teaching system suitable for the children of the golden future. He too carries an Ascension Flame and you can invoke it if you wish to do so. It would be particularly helpful for those who wish to teach or are already doing so. It would also help students. The only reason I did not include it in this trilogy of Ascension Flames is that Lord Kuthumi did not step forward to be part of it, whereas Lord Lanto, Lord Voosloo and Archangel Jophiel wanted to be part of the trilogy.

Lanto's Golden Flame of Wisdom through Compassion

Lord Lanto is the Master of the Second Ray of Love and Wisdom and the guardian of the Golden Ascension Flame of Wisdom through Compassion. He developed his heart centre to such an extent that golden Christ Light could be seen glowing through his skin.

Lord Voosloo's Ascension Flame of Universal Wisdom

Lord Voosloo originates from another universe. He was the highest-frequency High Priest ever to incarnate in Atlantis and enabled it to become a legendary civilization. His Flame of Universal Wisdom is a glorious sunshine yellow.

Archangel Jophiel's Flame of Cosmic Knowledge

Archangel Jophiel is an Angel of Wisdom. He is in charge of the crown chakra, the 1,000-petalled lotus that opens up to draw in universal knowledge and wisdom. His Flame is a transparent pale golden yellow.

VISUALIZATION TO BRING IN THE TRIPLE FLAMES OF KNOWLEDGE AND WISDOM

- Before you invoke these three Flames, breathe a few times into your third eye, then imagine that your third eye and crown chakra have merged into one big chakra.

- Lord Lanto appears before you with his Golden Flame of Wisdom through Compassion, which also has a hint of pink. He places it in your expanded third eye and crown centre. Let yourself relax as you feel it blazing in those chakras. Then it moves down to your heart.

- Then Lord Voosloo steps in front of you and you may gasp at the incredible high-frequency sunshine-yellow light he emanates. His sunshine-yellow Ascension Flame of Universal Wisdom holds the keys and codes that enabled Atlantis to make its incredible leap and will help our planet effect a double-dimensional shift into our next Golden Age. They will also accelerate your personal ascension. He now places the Flame in your third eye and crown, where it sparkles and shimmers. Then it moves down to your heart.

- Archangel Jophiel now floats down towards you with translucent pale yellow wings outstretched. In front of him he holds aloft his steady yellow Flame of Cosmic Knowledge. He gently places this yellow Flame into your third eye and crown chakras, where it radiates its light. And then it moves down to your heart.

- Quite suddenly, all three yellow Flames expand and engulf you, filling your cells with all the frequencies of cosmic knowledge and wisdom.

Cosmic Ascension Flames

As the name suggests, these are the most powerful Ascension Flames currently available to us. It is worth calling each one in individually to get accustomed to the energy in your fields. The triple combination will propel you up the ascension ladder and I would advise you use them with care and only after you have worked with the other Flames suggested in this book. They are powerful.

The Ascension Flame for the Perfected Human of the Golden Future

El Morya, the Manu or perfected human for the next root race of humanity, has a Flame that is red for vitality, blue for integrity and white for the White Brotherhood. White in this case stands for purity. This Flame holds the keys and codes for the next stage of human evolution, the beings we are all to become in the golden future, with our 12 strands of DNA connected and active.

Lord Hilarion's Flame of Wisdom and Higher Technology

Lord Hilarion is Master of the Fifth Ray of Science and Technology and his Flame is brilliant bright orange. As a planet, we are destined to receive downloads of spiritual technology that will take us beyond that used in the extraordinary civilization of Atlantis. This wondrous Flame holds the keys and codes of the next phase of our future evolution.

Archangel Metatron's Golden Orange Ascension Flame

Archangel Metatron is in charge of the ascension of humanity, the planet and the universe, and his Flame contains all that you will ever need for each step on your ascension path.

VISUALIZATION TO BRING IN THE TRIPLE COSMIC ASCENSION FLAMES

- First invoke El Morya and ask him to step forward with his vibrant red, blue and white Ascension Flame blazing. Know that it contains the blueprint of your perfected fifth-dimensional self. He holds it in front of you for a moment so that you can sense its power and importance as it throbs with energy. Then he steps forward and places it in your Stellar Gateway. You may not feel this, but it is starting to prepare you for the highest possibilities of the golden future.

- Lord Hilarion is wearing a brilliant orange cloak that matches the bright orange Ascension Flame of Wisdom and Higher Technology that he holds. The Flame is alive with the keys and codes of the spiritual technology of our golden future. You look into it for a long moment. Then Lord Hilarion places the great orange Flame in your Stellar Gateway.

- And now you may feel or see the mighty Archangel Metatron approach. He is enormous and you may sense that he is containing his light so that he does not overwhelm you. His golden orange Ascension Flame is glorious and full of sacred esoteric symbols. He places it with the others in your Stellar Gateway.

- After a few moments the three Flames start to move together down through your chakra system, igniting each centre with an ascension boost:

  - In your Soul Star chakra, they send their combined energy down the timeline of your past soul journey and then forward into the future to prepare you for a time beyond your comprehension or expectations.

- In your causal chakra, they open the doors to the angelic realms and call higher beings in to support you.

- In your crown chakra, they radiate into the universe with an invitation to download all that is for your highest good.

- In the third eye, their keys and codes unlock your higher gifts and powers.

- In your throat chakra, they open the gateway to higher communication and truth even wider.

- In your heart chakra, they all rest – the red, blue and white Flame of you as the perfected human with your 12 strands of DNA connected and active, the orange Flame of Wisdom and Higher Technology and the wondrous golden orange Ascension Flame. Take a moment to feel these three Flames burning and blazing in your heart, radiating light around you.

- In your solar plexus chakra, they expand this centre and enable you to pour out higher peace around the world.

- In your navel chakra, they blaze the future knowing of oneness into every continent.

- In your sacral chakra, they raise the frequency to transcendent love.

- In your base chakra, they create a fire so bright that everyone around you feels safe and looked after.

- In your Earth Star chakra, they dance and radiate, lighting up your potential and grounding this energy into your whole being.

Conclusion

We are moving towards a happy and spiritually enlightened future. All the things that I discuss in this book will happen, because the cosmic tide is bringing them forward. There will be new spiritual technology, a new health paradigm and golden communities. We will once more eat nutritionally rich, organic food and drink pure water. Golden cities will develop and we will communicate with animals and star beings. At last there will be world peace, international co-operation and freedom. This is inevitable. The flow of the universe is now activating the energy for the new Golden Age and the frequency everywhere is rising quickly.

However, every time you focus on the old ways and the challenges caused by the current collapse of society, you slow the transition and diminish the higher possibilities. Alternatively, every time you think about, talk about and visualize the amazing golden future awaiting us, you energize it for yourself and the collective. We all have so much more power than we give ourselves credit for. We are incredible at manifesting.

Here are some things you can do to bring forward the glorious golden future:

- Create a daily spiritual practice using the techniques in this book. Include the Rainbow Breath, Ascension Flames and, even better, triple Ascension Flames, and say the I AM mantras. Every time you do a spiritual exercise or practice, you raise not only your own frequency, but that of the collective consciousness and the planet.

- Work through the chambers of your chakras with the intention of mastering the lessons. Ask angels to help you do this and they will.

- Spend a little time each day visualizing the wonderful opportunities and new way of life opening up for us. When you focus on the joys of the golden future as if it is already here, magic happens. There are many visualizations in this book that you can use.

- Take the decisions to cut out of your life anything that focuses on the old paradigm.

- Spend time with people who are positive and orientated towards the golden future.

- Talk about the golden future and inspire others to think about it.

- Do more of everything that gives you joy and satisfaction.

As you do these things, watch your frequency rise and be aware of good things being attracted to your higher vibration.

Your soul chose to be on Earth during this period of monumental change. We are in it together, for it will be a time of community and oneness, so gather like-minded people around you to share and enjoy the journey.

Most important of all, make the golden future NOW.

Glossary

Abraham   Lord of Karma for the citrine 10th Ray of Peace; an aspect of El Morya; a great dragon master

Akashic Records   The storage place for all the details of a soul's journey over lifetimes

Akbar the Great   A wise ruler in India; an aspect of El Morya

Amethyst Crystal Skull   Fashioned in Atlantis, it contains the codes of all the knowledge accrued during the Golden Era of Atlantis.

Andromeda   A highly evolved galaxy holding love, peace and wisdom in equal measure

Angala, the birth of our planet   The first Golden Age on Earth

angelic beings   Beings on the angelic evolutionary line; these include elemental beings, angels on all frequencies and unicorns

Antakarana bridge   The bridge from your Soul Star to your Monad and then to Source

Aphrodite   A High Priestess of Love during the Golden Era of Atlantis

Apollo   A High Priest during the Golden Era of Atlantis

apportation   The ability to move objects to you

Archangels

- **Butyalil**   Pure white angel who ensures that the universe is working smoothly

- **Chamuel**   Pink Angel of Love who oversees the heart centre

- **Christiel**   White Angel of Peace who oversees the causal chakra, the unicorn kingdom and the stargate of Lyra

- **Gabriel**   White Angel of Purity and Joy who oversees the base, sacral and navel chakras

- **Hope**   Rainbow-coloured twin flame of Archangel Gabriel; she brings hope to humanity

- **Jophiel**   Pale gold Angel of Wisdom in charge of the crown chakra

- **Mallory**   Burgundy twin flame of Archangel Christiel and an Angel of Wisdom

- **Mariel**   Magenta angel in charge of the Soul Star chakra

- **Mary**   Aquamarine Angel of Love and Compassion, who overlit Mother Mary

- **Metatron**   Golden orange angel in charge of the Stellar Gateway chakra and the ascension of humanity and this universe

- **Michael**   Deep blue angel in charge of the throat chakra, who carries the Sword of Truth and the Shield of Protection

- **Purlimiek**   Green Angel of Nature

- **Raphael**   Emerald-green angel in charge of the third eye chakra of healing, enlightenment abundance and psychic development

- **Sandalphon**   Silver twin flame of Archangel Metatron, in charge of the Earth Star chakra and music

- **Uriel**   Directs the golden Angels of Peace; in charge of the solar plexus chakra

- **Zadkiel**   Violet Angel of Transmutation

Arcturus The beings from this star are advanced 10th-dimensional healers.

Arthur, King An aspect of El Morya

Ascension Flame A flame that holds light codes that are ninth-dimensional or higher to accelerate ascension

Ashtar Commander of the Intergalactic Fleet of starships that protect this universe

Athena A High Priestess of wisdom during the Golden Era of Atlantis

breatharian A person who lives on the *prana* in the air without food

Chakras

- **Earth Star chakra** Silver when fifth-dimensional; holds your divine potential

- **Base chakra** Platinum when fifth-dimensional; holds trust that you are divinely supported

- **Sacral chakra** Pale pink when fifth-dimensional; holds qualities of transcendent love

- **Navel chakra** Bright orange; holds codes of oneness

- **Solar plexus chakra** Gold when fifth-dimensional; holds self-worth, confidence, wisdom with power and divine majesty

- **Heart chakra** White when fifth-dimensional; holds codes of love

- **Throat chakra** Royal blue/teal when fifth-dimensional; holds codes of truth, honour, courage and strength

- **Alta Major chakra** Teal; it is the Seat of Consciousness within the throat chakra

- **Third eye chakra** Crystal green when fifth-dimensional; holds codes of enlightenment, abundance and psychic abilities

- **Crown chakra**   Crystal gold when fifth-dimensional; holds codes of cosmic connection

- **Causal chakra**   White; holds peace and angelic connection

- **Soul Star chakra**   Magenta; holds the information and wisdom of your soul

- **Stellar Gateway chakra**   Golden orange; holds the codes for ascension

Christ Light   Pure Source light containing knowledge and information

Christ love   Love directly from Source

claircogniscence   Divine knowing or *gnosis*

Cosmic Moment   A divine pause that took place at 11.11 a.m. on 21 December 2012

cosmic portal   Gateways to other dimensions that carry Christ Light

cosmic pyramids   Six pyramids built when Atlantis fell; cosmic computers programmed with the higher knowledge of the universe

Council for Planet Earth   The 12 Illumined Beings who take decisions for our planet

Council of Nine   An advanced group consciousness of nine beings in charge of Saturn

crystal skulls   Twelve computers each created from a single block of crystal in the shape of a human skull during the Golden Era of Atlantis. Each is programmed with the wisdom of the tribe where it was created.

crystalline brain   The brain structure that has the qualities of a crystal computer and will be the norm for the people of the golden future

Divine Feminine Contains all the qualities of the perfected feminine energy, such as love, compassion, nurturing, wisdom, intuition and enduring

Divine Masculine Contains all the qualities of the perfected masculine energy, such as strength, decision making, protective, thinking and quick changing

Djwhal Khul The Tibetan master who channelled through Alice Bailey. He was Casper, one of the three Wise Men. He is now the Master of Health through Harmony.

dolphins Wise ones of the planet; keepers of cosmic knowledge; holders of the knowledge and wisdom of the Golden Era of Atlantis

Druids Part of the White Brotherhood

El Morya A High Priest during the Golden Era of Atlantis. He is now the Manu, or perfected human, for the next spurt of human evolution; master of the First Ray of Power, Will and Purpose.

Elementals

- **elementals of air** Esaks, fairies, sylphs, air dragons

- **elementals of earth** Gnomes, goblins, pixies, earth dragons

- **elementals of water** Kyhils, mermaids, undines, water dragons

- **elementals of fire** Salamanders, fire dragons

- **elementals of wood** Warburtons

- **elementals with combined elements** Dragons, fauns, imps

Gaia, Lady The angel in charge of our planet

Gautama, Lord The first person on this planet to become the Buddha, the embodiment of wisdom and peace

golden cities Ecological communities built for the benefit of all the inhabitants and radiating a golden aura

Golden Era of Atlantis   A 1,500-year period during the fifth and last experiment of Atlantis, during which the people maintained a fifth-dimensional vibration and led idyllic lives

Great Crystal of Atlantis   The vast crystal that provided the power for Atlantis from pure Source energy

guardian angel   The angelic being designated to accompany you throughout your life

Halls of Amenti   A library in Hollow Earth containing the records of all the masters in the cosmos

Harmonic Convergence   A planetary alignment in 1987 that marked the 25-year purification period before 2012

Helios   Known as the Great Central Sun, a gateway to Source, where the Codes of Light for this universe are created by Archangel Metatron.

Hermes   A High Priest during the Golden Era of Atlantis; his tribe later became the kahunas in Hawaii, taking the *Ho'oponopono* prayer with them.

Hilarion   Originally from Sirius, a negotiator for Earth on the Council of Saturn; he is bringing forward spiritual technology for the New Age.

Hollow Earth   The seventh-dimensional chakra in the centre of our planet

Ho'oponopono   Huna healing prayer: 'I am sorry. Please forgive me. Thank you. I love you.'

Horus   A High Priest during the Golden Era of Atlantis

illumined ones   Those who have mastered the lessons of Earth and carry a high percentage of light

Imhotep   A High Priest during the Golden Era of Atlantis

Intergalactic Council   The 12 mighty beings who take decisions for this universe

Isis   A High Priestess in the Golden Era of Atlantis

Jesus   The illumined one who brought the Christ Light to Earth; the Bringer of Cosmic Love

Jupiter   The planet of expansion and abundance

Knights Templar   Part of the White Brotherhood

Kumeka   Master of the topaz Eighth Ray of Deep Cleansing Transformation, Joy and Oneness

kundalini of Earth   The life-force energy of our planet

Kuthumi   The World Teacher

Lake Atitlan   The etheric retreat in South America of Archangel Sandalphon

Lanto   Master of the Second Ray of Love and Wisdom

Lemuria   The fourth Golden Age, the one that preceded Atlantis, known for oneness and love of nature

levitation   The ability to control your energy fields so that you can transport yourself to a different location

lightworker   A soul who is consciously working for the light

Lyra   The stargate to the unicorn kingdom, overseen by Archangel Christiel

mage   A powerful priest or priestess who worked with the High Priests and Priestesses of Atlantis; plural *magi*

manifestation   The ability to draw objects to you from the invisible realms

Marko   From Saturn; he represents the highest galactic confederation in our solar system.

Mars   The beings from this planet help to keep the universe in order.

Mary Magdalene   In charge of the Sixth Ray of Loving, Devoted Service, bringing the influence of the Divine Feminine into religion; she is also bringing in new healing methods.

Mary, Mother   The mother of Jesus; the master of love and compassion

Melchior   One of the three Wise Men; he forecast the time and place of Jesus' birth; an aspect of El Morya

Merlin   An aspect of St Germain; represents the Council of Saturn

Metatron Cube   The sacred symbol of Archangel Metatron, containing all the sacred geometry for ascension

Mind control   Mastery of your thoughts so that you can control your energy fields

Monad   Your original divine spark from Source, your 12th-dimensional light; known as your I AM Presence

Moon   Holds the Divine Feminine qualities of the universe

Mu   The third Golden Age on Earth, preceding Lemuria; in the Pacific

Music of the Spheres   The harmonics created by the movement of the stars and planets

Nada, Lady   An illumined master with no ego; Master of the Seventh Ray bringing forward sacred wisdom, and Lord of Karma of the Third Ray

Neptune   The planet of higher spirituality

Nigellay   The aspect of Mars that has ascended and carries the quality of spiritual leadership

Orion   Constellation of wisdom that has already ascended

out-breath of God   Ten cosmic eras covering 260,000 years

Pallas Athena   The goddess of truth; Lord of Karma of the Fourth Ray of Harmony and Balance

Paul the Venetian   A High Priest in the Golden Era of Atlantis; holds the Flame of Freedom

Peter the Great   Lord of Karma of the 11th Ray of Clarity, Mysticism and Healing; he is very in tune with nature and animals.

Petranium   The second Golden Age on Earth, in Africa

Pleiades   A seventh-dimensional star system carrying blue heart-healing light

Poseidon   A High Priest in the Golden Era of Atlantis

Quan Yin   A High Priestess in the Golden Era of Atlantis; had a 2,000-year incarnation in China and is a goddess of love

Ra   A High Priest in the Golden Era of Atlantis

Rakoczy   An incarnation of St Germain; Master of the 11th Ray of Clarity, Mysticism and Healing; helping humans to accept the changing energies

Rosicrucians   The Order of the Rosy Cross; a branch of the Great White Brotherhood

St Catherine of Siena   Lord of Karma for the 12th Ray of Unconditional Love; helping religions to become more spiritual

St Clare of Assisi   An ascended master of the higher hierarchy bringing spiritual awareness to humanity

St Germain   The Keeper of the Golden Scales and Lord of Civilization, as well as the Master of the Violet Ray, the Seventh Ray of Ritual, Ceremony and Magic

St Teresa of Avila   An ascended master helping to bring religions together for the new Golden Age

Sanat Kumara Has returned to Venus, but still helps us with our ascension process; he used to hold the kundalini of the planet in the Gobi Desert as a masculine energy. In 2008, the Mayan elders moved it to Archangel Sandalphon's retreat at Lake Atitlan in South America.

Saturn The planet of discipline and control

Sentinels of Anubis Protect the records in the Halls of Amenti

Seraphim Highest-frequency angels who surround the Godhead, singing in creation

Seraphina A Seraphim who engages with humanity; presides with Archangel Metatron over the Stellar Gateway chakra and oversees the Intergalactic Training Schools

Serapis Bey A High Priest in the Golden Era of Atlantis; Master of the Fourth Ray, the Ray of Harmony and Balance; the only master to work with the Seraphim; Keeper of the White Ascension Flame

Sett A High Priest during the Golden Era of Atlantis

Silver Ray The Divine Feminine Ray

Sirius Beings from the star Sirius are bringing in spiritual technology; Christ Light is held here at a ninth-dimensional frequency. The part that has ascended is Lakumay, where a Golden Globe holds Christ Light at an 11th-dimensional frequency.

Solomon, King An aspect of El Morya

soul Your Higher Self, holding all your knowledge and wisdom

Sphinx, the The guardian of our planet

spiritual hierarchy The spiritual beings who look after our universe

star beings Etheric beings who inhabit the stellar world

Sun Holds the codes of the Divine Masculine and happiness

teleportation   The ability to disappear and move to a different place

Thoth   A High Priest during the Golden Era of Atlantis

Veil of Amnesia   The seven layers that shroud our third eye from seeing our true divinity

Venus   The planet of love, known as the Cosmic Heart

Venus, Lady   A High Priestess of the Temple of Love in Atlantis; a goddess of love

Violet Flame   The violet-coloured Flame of Transmutation held by St Germain and Archangel Zadkiel

Voosloo, Lord   The highest-frequency High Priest to incarnate in Atlantis; he enabled the civilization to jump-shift into the Golden Age it became. He is now the Master of the Ninth Ray, the yellow Ray of Harmony, which entered the planet in 2001 and balances the mind and spirit of humanity. In contrast, the Fourth Ray brings about harmony and balance on an amethyst and white vibration.

White Brotherhood   A group of highly evolved orders who radiate white light and hold the secrets of peace and purity. They include the Cathars, Druids, Essenes, Rosicrucians and others; part of the Great White Brotherhood.

Zeus   A High Priest during the Golden Era of Atlantis

Toby Phillips

About the Author

Diana Cooper received an angel visitation during a time of personal crisis. She is now well known for her work with angels, Orbs, Atlantis, unicorns, ascension and the transition to the new Golden Age. Through her guides and angels she enables people to access their spiritual gifts and psychic potential, and also connects them to their own angels, guides, Masters and unicorns.

Diana is the founder of The Diana Cooper Foundation, a not-for-profit organization that offers certificated spiritual teaching courses throughout the world. She is also the bestselling author of 34 books, which have been published in 28 languages.

www.dianacooper.com

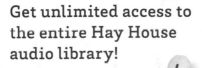

CONNECT WITH
HAY HOUSE
ONLINE

 hayhouse.co.uk   **f** @hayhouse

 @hayhouseuk   @hayhouseuk

 @hayhouseuk   @hayhouseuk

Find out all about our latest books & card decks • *Be the first to know about exclusive discounts* • *Interact with our authors in live broadcasts* • *Celebrate the cycle of the seasons with us* • *Watch free videos from your favourite authors* • *Connect with like-minded souls*

'The gateways to wisdom and knowledge are always open.'

Louise Hay